CONVERSATIONS
WITH SCRIPTURE:
THE GOSPEL
OF LUKE

Other Books in the Series

CONVERSATIONS
WITH SCRIPTURE:

THE GOSPEL
OF LUKE

FREDERICK W. SCHMIDT

Morehouse Publishing
NEW YORK · HARRISBURG · DENVER

Morehouse Publishing, 4775 Linglestown Road, Harrisburg, PA 17112

Morehouse Publishing, 445 Fifth Avenue, New York, NY 10016

Morehouse Publishing is an imprint of Church Publishing Incorporated.

Cover art: Icon by the hand of Judy Cole, entitled "St. Luke." For further information about the iconographer, see: www.jcoleicons.com

Series cover design by Corey Kent

Series design by Beth Oberholtzer

Library of Congress Cataloging-in-Publication Data

Schmidt, Frederick W.
    Conversations with Scripture : the Gospel of Luke / Frederick W. Schmidt.
        p.   cm. — (Anglican Association of Biblical Scholars study series)
    Includes bibliographical references.
    ISBN 978-0-8192-2361-6 (pbk.)
    1. Bible. N.T. Luke—Criticism, interpretation, etc. I. Title.
BS2595.52.S36   2009
226.4'06—dc22
                                                                    2009032060

Printed in the United States of America

09 10 11 12 13 14   10 9 8 7 6 5 4 3 2 1

For Natalie

And In Memoriam
Robert W. Lyon
George Bradford Caird
Who lived and taught their passion

Almighty God, who inspired your servant Luke the physician to set forth in the gospel the love and healing power of your Son: Graciously continue in your Church this love and power to heal, to the praise and glory of your Name; through Jesus Christ our Lord, who lives and reigns with you, in the unity of the Holy Spirit, one God, now and for ever.

AMEN[1]

CONTENTS

INTRODUCTION
TO THE SERIES

To talk about a distinctively Anglican approach to Scripture is a daunting task. Within any one part of the larger church that we call the Anglican Communion there is, on historical grounds alone, an enormous variety. But as the global character of the church becomes apparent in ever-newer ways, the task of accounting for that variety, while naming the characteristics of a distinctive approach becomes increasingly difficult.

In addition, the examination of Scripture is not confined to formal studies of the kind addressed in this series of parish studies written by formally trained biblical scholars. Systematic theologian David Ford, who participated in the Lambeth Conference of 1998, rightly noted that although "most of us have studied the Bible over many years" and "are aware of various academic approaches to it," we have "also lived in it" and "inhabited it, through worship, preaching, teaching and meditation." As such, Ford observes, "The Bible in the Church is like a city we have lived in for a long time." We may not be able to account for the history of every building or the architecture on every street, but we know our way around and it is a source of life to each of us.[2]

That said, we have not done as much as we should in acquainting the inhabitants of that famed city with the architecture that lies within. So, as risky as it may seem, it is important to set out an introduction to the highlights of that city—which this series proposes to explore at length. Perhaps the best way in which to broach that task is to provide a handful of descriptors.

The first of those descriptors that leaps to mind is familiar, basic, and forever debated: *authoritative.* Years ago I was asked by a colleague who belonged to the Evangelical Free Church why someone with as much obvious interest in the Bible would be an Episcopal priest. I responded, "Because we read the whole of Scripture and not just the parts of it that suit us." Scripture has been and continues to play a singular role in the life of the Anglican Communion, but it has rarely been used in the sharply prescriptive fashion that has characterized some traditions.

Some have characterized this approach as an attempt to navigate a *via media* between overbearing control and an absence of accountability. But I think it is far more helpful to describe the tensions not as a matter of steering a course between two different and competing priorities, but as the complex dance necessary to live under a very different, but typically Anglican notion of authority itself. Authority shares the same root as the word "to author" and as such, refers first and foremost, not to the *power* to *control* with all that both of those words suggest, but to the capacity to *author creativity*, with all that both of those words suggest.[3] As such, the function of Scripture is to carve out a creative space in which the work of the Holy Spirit can yield the very kind of fruit associated with its work in the church. The difficulty, of course, is that for that space to be creative, it is also necessary for it to have boundaries, much like the boundaries we establish for other kinds of genuinely creative freedom—the practice of scales for concert pianists, the discipline of work at the barre that frees the ballerina, or the guidance that parents provide for their children. Defined in this way, it is possible to see the boundaries around that creative space as barriers to be eliminated, or as walls that provide protection, but they are neither.

And so the struggle continues with the authority of Scripture. From time to time in the Anglican Communion, it has been and will be treated as a wall that protects us from the complexity of navigating without error the world in which we live. At other times, it will be treated as the ancient remains of a city to be cleared away in favor of a brave new world. But both approaches are rooted, not in the limitations of Scripture, but in our failure to welcome the creative space we have been given.

For that reason, at their best, Anglican approaches to Scripture are also *illuminative*. William Sloane Coffin once observed that the problem with Americans and the Bible is that we read it like a drunk uses a lamppost. We lean on it, we don't use it for illumination.[4] Leaning on Scripture—or having the lamppost taken out completely—are simply two very closely related ways of failing to acknowledge the creative space provided by Scripture. But once the creative space is recognized for what it is, then the importance of reading Scripture illuminatively becomes apparent. Application of the insight Scripture provides into who we are and what we might become is not something that can be prescribed or mapped out in detail. It is only a conversation with Scripture, marked by humility, that can begin to spell out the particulars. Reading Scripture is, then, in the Anglican tradition a delicate and demanding task, that involves both the careful listening for the voice of God and courageous conversation with the world around us.

It is, for that reason, an approach that is also marked by *critical engagement* with the text itself. It is no accident that from 1860 to 1900 the three best-known names in the world of biblical scholarship were Anglican priests, the first two of whom were bishops: B. F. Westcott, J. B. Lightfoot, and F. J. A. Hort. Together the three made contributions to both the church and the critical study of the biblical text that became a defining characteristic of Anglican life.

Of the three, Westcott's contribution, perhaps, best captures the balance. Not only did his work contribute to a critical text of the Greek New Testament that would eventually serve as the basis for the English Revised Version, but as Bishop of Durham he also convened a conference of Christians to discuss the arms race in Europe, founded the Christian Social Union, and mediated the Durham coal strike of 1892.

The English roots of the tradition are not the only, or even the defining characteristic of Anglican approaches to Scripture. The church, no less than the rest of the world, has been forever changed by the process of globalization, which has yielded a rich *diversity* that complements the traditions once identified with the church.

Scripture in Uganda, for example, has been read with an emphasis on private, allegorical, and revivalist applications. The result has been a tradition in large parts of East Africa that stresses the reading of Scripture on one's own; the direct application made to the contemporary situation without reference to the setting of the original text; and the combination of personal testimony with the power of public exhortation.

At the same time, however, globalization has brought that tradition into conversation with people from other parts of the Anglican Communion as the church in Uganda has sought to bring the biblical text to bear on its efforts to address the issues of justice, poverty, war, disease, food shortage, and education. In such a dynamic environment, the only thing that one can say with certainty is that neither the Anglican Communion, nor the churches of East Africa, will ever be the same again.

Authoritative, illuminative, critical, and varied—these are not the labels that one uses to carve out an approach to Scripture that can be predicted with any kind of certainty. Indeed, if the word *dynamic*—just used—is added to the list, perhaps all that one can predict is still more change! And, for that reason, there will be observers who (not without reason) will argue that the single common denominator in this series is that each of the authors also happens to be an Anglican. (There might even be a few who will dispute that!)

But such is the nature of life in any city, including one shaped by the Bible. We influence the shape of its life, but we are also shaped and nurtured by it. And if that city is of God's making, then to force our own design on the streets and buildings around us is to disregard the design that the chief architect has in mind.

—Frederick W. Schmidt
Series Editor

AUTOBIOGRAPHICAL NOTE

Knowledge saves us on condition that it engages all that we are: only when it constitutes a way which works and transforms, and which wounds our nature as the plough wounds the soil. This is to say that intelligence and metaphysical certainty alone do not save, and do not of themselves prevent titanic falls.

—FRITHJOF SCHUON[5]

Teaching both New Testament studies and spiritual formation for nearly a decade has changed the way in which I view the biblical text. As the reader will gather from the first chapter, I remain convinced that solid historical and exegetical work is the surest guarantee that the text will speak for itself—as both a revelatory and authoritative text. Though, heaven knows, that is all that human endeavor can bring to the task of liberating "the word of the Lord." Much more depends—and decisively so—upon the work of the Holy Spirit.

So many of the convictions that shaped my earlier work remain intact. But after moving between the two obligations that have shaped my academic work of late, I have become convinced that an approach to the biblical text that eschews questions of its relevance or runs roughshod over its significance by either ignoring the differences between then and now, or by impugning its value, are worse than useless.

The church and the people of God are particularly ill-served by the two brands of fundamentalism that lurk behind these abuses. On the one side is the widely acknowledged fundamentalism of the right. On that side of the equation are scholars who ignore the complexities of the text's character, the distance of millennia, and the attendant differences between our own setting and that of every biblical text. Armed with certainty and a commitment to making Scripture speak to the contemporary believer, all they actually accomplish is the naïve, if not cynical credentialing of their own views.

There is, however, a fundamentalism of the left. It is often populated by *unrecovered* fundamentalists—a breed of scholar who often began his or her pilgrimage as a fundamentalist of the right, assumed that they could "prove" God, and defended a narrow understanding of Christianity by ignoring the tough business of attending to the voice of Scripture, intent on making it say what they believe it needed to say. Once they were liberated from this narrow provincialism, they did what so many of us do. They swung, pendulum-like, to the opposite and equally provincial conclusion, arguing that because Scripture could not be made to say what it should say, it had nothing to say of any enduring spiritual significance.

What neither side is willing to acknowledge is how much they share by way of presupposition. The net result is a religious and spiritual dialog (in this country, at least) that is marked by a debate over false and unworkable alternatives: know-nothings who eschew the academy and atheists who champion themselves as the spokespersons for the truth.

The alternative, it seems to me, represents the best of traditions in the church: a commitment to Scripture that is confident of its power as the Word of God, scholarship that is confident that the fullest exploration of Scripture best serves the church, and contemplation of its meaning that weds the two. However imperfectly, it is my hope that this brief commentary will thread the needle between the lackluster and death-dealing alternatives and offer something inspired by the better instincts of the Anglican and Episcopal tradition.[6]

INTRODUCTION

Sociologists observe that we as human beings create our own worlds. We thread together realities that define our relationship with the people and things around us. In turn, that definition takes on a life of its own, making its demands upon us and shaping our lives. We create a world and the world creates us.[7]

Some would define that process as proof that our convictions about God have no more reality than the social needs that give them shape. The same argument was made when we began to analyze the scientific and psychological dimensions of our lives. Each time we have made discoveries of this kind someone has suggested that our religious and spiritual convictions are the product of scientific, psychological, or social necessity.

The problem with such sweeping claims is that the physical, psychological, and social dimensions of life are part, but they are not all, of what it means to be human; and simply because our needs share psychological and social characteristics does not make them any less real. Our lives have spiritual, aesthetic, and altruistic dimensions that transcend bodily processes or psychological and social needs. They are more than the sum total of their parts.[8]

We can conclude otherwise, of course. We can embrace the conviction that the natural forces at work in our world are all there is to it. But the price of that conviction is nihilism: the conviction that our lives mean nothing and can never mean anything.

By contrast, the genius of the Jewish and Christian traditions has been the willingness to acknowledge the goodness of all that it means to be human—including the physical, chemical, psychological, and social processes that mark our existence. The conviction of both traditions has been that God works in and through them. They have resisted denying their reality or arguing that we utterly transcend them; and, with equally good reason, they have argued that human life—because God is its creator—amounts to more than the sum total of its parts.

Christianity is an incarnational faith—we believe in a God who takes on human form. We believe in a church led by the Holy Spirit that occupies the historical and physical realm as an embodied expression of God's will for the world.

Luke would have used different terms, but I am convinced that he believed the same thing. To belong to the church of Jesus Christ—to hear the story of God's saving work in and through the children of Israel, beginning with Moses and the prophets—was also a matter of belonging, naming a tradition, relating to the creative space within it that is its authority, finding new hope, and living into an obligation to behave in new ways. It is around those needs that this interpretation of Luke's gospel revolves.

It is difficult to nurture the mystery of an incarnational gift like the one that Luke celebrates in a culture that so easily confuses its ability to describe something with the ability to control it or explain it away. My prayer is that the reflections outlined here will prompt at least a few readers to pause and recognize the mystery that is the presence of the resurrected and glorified Christ in the story that we share.

CHAPTER ONE

Telling the Old, Old Story

Luke had a story to tell and he told his story to change people's lives.

If you have ever worked with a therapist or a spiritual director, you know how important stories can be. The best of therapists and directors rely upon storytelling. They tell their own stories. They tell stories about other people. Most important of all, they rely on the storytelling skills of their clients. Getting them to tell their stories is what finally makes the difference.

The Primal Need for Stories

Stories help us to remember our past. They help us to make sense of new events in our lives; and, when we are stuck or confused, they help us to imagine where we go next.

Think, for example, of the story that explains how you overcame a significant life challenge. Perhaps you suffered an injury or illness, or at some point in your life you lost a job. The chances are the story has chapters and turning points. There were important things said by someone who loves you or advises you. You discovered a new insight that

Luke had a story to tell and he told his story to change people's lives.

changed the way in which you viewed your circumstances or managed the challenge you faced. Whatever the details, there were elements of the past, the present, and the future involved.

What is interesting about stories of this kind is that they not only help us to recount the past, they help us to imagine a way forward. Until we've told our story, we are often at a loss to know how to go on. We live uneasily with the stuck-place we find ourselves in and we can drift through days on end without making any progress. It is only when we wrap a story around what has happened to us that we can tell to others that we can imagine a new chapter that begins with the words, "And then . . ."

Luke did not know anything about modern therapy or spiritual direction, and he hardly would have described the value of stories in the terms that I have used. But the power of stories to change our lives does not depend upon modern theories. Their power arises out of a far more primal and human need; that need accounts for the universal presence of stories across time, cultures, and races. This description is more an effort to bring to the surface what we intuitively know about those stories.

Luke knew this too. He understood the need to recount the past, to put it in order. He knew that this kind of storytelling helped to explain the present. And he knew that if he could do that, he could also describe the future. Addressing the needs of other Christians, he used the stories he had heard told about the ministry of Jesus to help his circle in the ancient church understand where they had been, where they were, and where they were going.

Addressing the needs of other Christians, Luke used the stories he had heard told about the ministry of Jesus to help his circle in the ancient church understand where they had been, where they were, and where they were going.

The staying power of those stories led the church to read and re-read his gospel, copy it, and eventually treat it as sacred Scripture. Millennia later Luke's stories still shape our lives and the life of the church; and therein lays both the gift and the challenge of reading Luke's gospel.

Basic Elements of Storytelling

Stories—ancient, as well as modern—are never told in a vacuum. Their shape, content, and focus depend upon the environment in which they are told. The four basic elements of that environment include:

- The storyteller
- The circle of listeners to whom the story was told
- The circumstances under which the stories were told
- And the events that prompted the storytelling

When someone first tells a story, those basic elements are taken for granted by both the storyteller and the people who hear it. Imagine, for example, the stories told around your family dinner table. Everyone knows Uncle Robert and remembers the pipe he smoked. The way he gestured with it to make a point; the smell of the cheap tobacco he used. You can see Aunt Martha in your mind's eye—her quick wit, the ready smile. You can even smell the gingerbread she made for family gatherings.

So when you start telling the stories of the fishing trip they took to New Mexico, no one needs to fill in the blanks. The storyteller and the listeners know one another; and both know the circumstances under which the stories were told and the events that prompted the original telling of the story.

But as time passes, the common elements that made that kind of storytelling possible are not as readily obvious. As communities grow, circumstances change, and generations pass, the identity of the storyteller and the first audience is often lost to us. It is harder to know what concerned or interested them, or what first prompted someone to tell a story.

People, places, circumstances, and cultures can and do completely change. With them the original meanings of stories can be lost as well. Even the details about Uncle Robert's pipe and Aunt Martha's gingerbread can be lost.

This is not to say that there are not enduring themes and common human characteristics that continue to shine through the oldest of stories. Bible stories, Aesop's fables, even a story about Uncle Robert can still entertain or teach us some-

The broader meaning of ancient stories often tempts us to forget how different our world is from the one in which the original storyteller lived.

thing. For that reason we can almost always get some kind of meaning out of a story, and it's that broader meaning that often tempts us to forget how different our world is from the one in which the original storyteller lived.

For example, I teach a class that introduces students to the basics of monastic spirituality. As a part of the work that the students are asked to do, we often read the stories of the ancient desert fathers and mothers whose lives of devotion gave rise to the early monasteries. One of the ancient stories told runs this way:

> Some old men went to Abba Poemen and asked, "If we see brothers sleeping during the common prayer, should we wake them?"
>
> Abba Poemen answered, "If I see my brother sleeping, I put his head on my knees and let him rest."
>
> Then one old man spoke up, "And how do you explain yourself before God?"
>
> Abba Poemen replied, "I say to God: You have said, 'First take the beam out of your own eye and then you will be able to remove the splinter from the eye of your brother.'"[9]

Left to their own devices, my students will often conclude that the story tells them something about the level of comfort they might experience in prayer; the importance of acknowledging their frailty—even when engaged in spiritual pursuits; and something rather more general about the importance of avoiding a judgmental spirit. But the story was probably told and retold in its original setting as a means of shaping the way in which individual monks treated one another in the close confines of monastic community. In turn, their concern about how they treated one another was rooted in an understanding of community shaped by waiting and preparing spiritually for the return of Christ that required them to set aside every other care. So the story has a context and point of application that, more often than not, my students completely miss at first.

When it comes to reading stories, then, there is almost always some kind of meaning that can be derived from hearing one, even if you don't know why the person who originally told the story chose to tell it or the point they intended to make. But there is also a lot that can be missed.

If we are reading a story to be entertained, that is not necessarily a bad thing. We may want nothing more than to lose ourselves for a time in the story that is told—to laugh, to cry, to reminisce. Reading a story without reference to what it was originally intended to communicate can also be spiritually beneficial. My students often learned things from the stories they read from the desert fathers and mothers, even when they didn't understand their original intention.

Stories as Mirrors and Windows

But they also missed things they could benefit from hearing, and that is the problem with an approach to biblical stories that never asks, "What did the original storyteller have in mind?" When we read Scripture, we are trying to hear more than the stories we would tell ourselves. We are looking for deeper truths and fresh insights into our lives. We are looking for more than the stories we can hear from our cultural, historical, or personal perspective.

We often miss things we could benefit from hearing when we fail to ask, "What did the original storyteller have in mind?"

Even more boldly—as the words of our liturgy affirm—we are listening for "the word of the Lord." That, in part, is what we mean when we describe Scripture as God's revelation to us. When we fail to ever ask what the storyteller might have originally meant, we foreclose on an important part of that revelation; and we run the risk of assuming that the way we hear the story is all there is to it.

One way to understand the difference is to think of windows and mirrors. If we listen to the story as it was told, Scripture functions like a window into another world. We see the issues an ancient audience faced; the struggle they experienced; and the hopes they embraced. We also discover that our own way of framing life's challenges is not the one and only way to understand the world around us. When we open ourselves up to those differences, the stories of Scripture have the power to challenge, comfort, and provoke us in ways we never expected. The subtle differences challenge our assumptions.

If we listen to the story as it was told, Scripture functions like a window into another world. But if we ignore its intended meaning, then Scripture functions like a mirror. We hear (and see) little more than what we already know.

But if we ignore its intended meaning, then Scripture functions like a mirror. We hear (and see) little more than what we already know and we interpose our own story on the story Scripture offers to tell. What is lost as a result? The ability to hear something more—a new chapter, a different path, an unexpected ending—and without that, we lose the ability to grow and change.

The Gospel of the Lord

If reading Scripture were simply a matter of self-improvement, perhaps it would not matter so much. In the course of life, we all have more than one kind of opportunity to learn, and it is difficult to take advantage of all those opportunities. But when we read Luke, we claim that his story is "the gospel of the Lord." It is clearly far more than just another opportunity to grow. It is the word of the Lord.

The failure to ask those questions is not unique to any one theological point of view. People on the "left" as well as the "right" of most theological questions can be supremely confident that their truth is the biblical truth, and fundamentalism has no single home.

And truth be told, most of us have difficulty remaining open to the voice of Scripture when it cuts across our lives at odd angles. A friend of mine who is an editor for a major publisher notes that most people buy nonfiction books to reinforce opinions they already hold by reading the experts who agree with them, rather than to challenge themselves. The same is true of the Bible. Most people use it to reinforce the point of view they already hold. But more often than not there are subtle, if not profound differences between the storyteller's world and ours that makes such easy use of the Bible all but impossible.

This has been a particular problem as it applies to Luke's gospel. Scholars who have ignored the original import of Luke's story have treated his gospel as if it were a dramatization of the Apostle's Creed, ignoring the subtle differences between the message of Luke and the first four centuries of the church's theological development. Some have seen it as the "gospel of inclusion," ignoring the fact that Luke could not have comprehended the contemporary political overtones of that phrase; others as the story of Jesus the Marxist, ignoring the vast differences between first-century Palestine and modern economies. Some of those readings of Luke traipse across more centuries than others, but all three of them ignore just how impossible it is to claim that Luke thought in those categories.

The challenge, of course, is to identify the basic elements that shaped Luke's original telling of the story. Who was the original storyteller? Who was a part of the original circle of listeners? What was happening when the story was originally told? What circumstances prompted the original storytelling? Fortunately, we actually know a great deal.

It is admittedly harder to know precisely what Luke meant. There is educated "guesswork" involved; and making the connections between the challenges that Luke faced and those we face is more like triangulation than it is application. But, by contrast, an approach to biblical stories that strives to hear them as they were told opens up the possibility for Scripture to stand on its own and tell us something we might not have otherwise heard.

The challenge is to identify the basic elements that shaped Luke's original telling of the story. Who was the original storyteller? Who was a part of the original circle of listeners? What was happening when the story was originally told? What circumstances prompted the original storytelling?

The Storyteller

Broadly speaking, there are two opinions about who "the Luke" of Luke's gospel might have been.

One group of scholars believes that the writer is well-educated and the product of a Greek education, but otherwise unknown to us. They base their view on the content of the gospel, which contains very little of an explicit kind that would identify the author. That's not at all uncommon in ancient storytelling. Ancient books did not contain a title page, book spine, or Library of Congress catalog number, so the writer had to identify himself for us to know who he was and Luke does not do that. So most of the scholars who take this position point to the writer's proficiency with Greek, the nature of his word choice, and his facility with the literary forms of the day. They set aside the traditions about the authorship of the gospel that circulated in the early church as too late to be of real value.

Other scholars give greater weight to those traditions and believe that Luke was a physician and companion to the Apostle Paul. For them the convincing evidence lies at the intersection of four kinds of evidence:

Broadly speaking, there are two opinions about who "the Luke" of Luke's gospel might have been.

- The ascription (or title) added to the gospel describing it as Luke's work (which probably dates to 175 CE)
- The reference made in more than one piece of literature from the early church that describes the gospel as Luke's work (which date between 170 and 208 CE)
- The references made in the New Testament epistles to Luke, a physician and Paul's companion (Phlm 24; Col 4:14; 2 Tim 4:11)
- And the references to first-person experiences in the book of Acts, which scholars widely agree was also written by the author of the third gospel (Acts 16:10–17; 20:5–15; 21:1–18; 27:1–28:16).

Church traditions on matters of authorship should not be accepted at face value. Such claims evolved slowly and informally. They probably circulated orally long before they found their way into print anywhere. It is all but impossible to know where they originated and by modern standards such claims were hardly scrutinized closely. (Although it is easy to overestimate how exacting "modern standards" are.)

By the same token, such claims should not be rejected out of hand. Assuming that the gospel was written around 85 CE, the tradition about Luke's authorship may be as little as eighty-five years old, and if the written claim did circulate by word of mouth (and it no doubt did), then it may have been accepted thinking much closer to the time of the gospel's original composition.

Church traditions on matters of authorship should not be accepted at face value. By the same token, such claims should not be rejected out of hand.

The random mix of third person ("they") and first person ("we") language in the book of Acts would also make a lot more sense if one of Paul's companions was the original storyteller. As some scholars suggest, moving back and forth between the two kinds of language could be attributed to an older man (like the writer of the gospel) reflecting back on his experiences as a younger man (like Luke, Paul's companion). The language in Acts could also be attributed to the perspective of someone who witnessed some of the changes in the church, but not all of them, and who was scrupulous about observing the difference when telling the story. "*We* did this

(I know because I was there.). *They* did that (I wasn't there, but I heard about it.)."

In the end, it may not make a great deal of difference what one concludes about the authorship of the gospel and both views are necessarily a matter of educated guesswork. What is clear is that:

- The writer was a Gentile, not a Jew.
- He had a Greek education.
- He knew a lot about the ministry of Jesus and the circumstances in first-century Palestine.
- He knew a lot about Judaism and about what mattered to Jews. And it is the only kind of learning you do by being a God-fearer.[10]
- He was broadly familiar with the challenges the fledgling church was facing.
- And he was deeply interested in addressing the issues raised for the church's increasingly Gentile constituency.

> *If the writer was not the Luke whom Paul knew, the author was undoubtedly someone like him.*

If the writer was not the Luke whom Paul knew, the author was undoubtedly someone like him.

The Original Circle of Listeners

Luke's original circle of listeners is also important to understanding what the story meant to those who heard it. Like the storyteller, they were undoubtedly Gentiles.

The "Theophilus" to whom the gospel is addressed could be an individual (Luke 1:3). Some scholars have suggested that he might have even commissioned the writing of the gospel. But it is hard to imagine the circumstances under which this kind of commission might have been given at this early stage in the church's life. Others believe that the adjectives "most excellent" mean that he was a Roman official. What is more likely is that Theophilus, whose name is plainly Greek in origin and means "lover of God," is a surrogate for a group of readers: "To all you most excellent lovers of God . . ."

> **Gentile:** A non-Jew.

What is less clear is where Luke's audience lived. Some scholars have tried to identify a single church to which the gospel was written.

The ancient congregation in Antioch, for example, is often identified as a possibility. But there is no reliable information in the stories that Luke tells to prove that is the case.

Given the breadth of its appeal to Gentile Christians, it seems far more likely that while the gospel was necessarily read in one place at first, the story itself was written with the widespread Gentile audience that was scattered around the Mediterranean in mind. In that regard, Luke's original audience probably looked a lot like the converts that the book of Acts eventually describes and may well account for its wider use and popularity in the early church.

It is also important to remember that Luke's audience was a circle of listeners, not readers.

It is also important to remember that Luke's audience was a circle of *listeners*, not *readers*. He wrote his gospel to be read aloud. It is not a piece of writing to be pored over or analyzed word by word, as we so often do today. Formal education was not available on a broad basis, very few people could read or write, and the cultures of the ancient world reproduced books by hand.

This is not to say that Luke and his audience were primitive, simple, or lacking in intelligence, but it does mean that even those who could write relied upon oral communication to spread their stories and ideas. Reproducing books for those who could read was both slow and expensive. For that reason, anthropologists describe the culture in which Luke wrote as "preliterary"—a culture in which a few people did all of the reading and writing for everyone else. It is little wonder, then, that Luke used the drama of stories, the sweep of the narrative, and repetition to communicate with his audience. Stories rule when you are listening, instead of reading. They are easier to hear, see, understand, and remember.

Preliterary: a culture in which a few people do all of the reading and writing for everyone else.

The Original Circumstances

Luke and his audience lived in a complicated world and a fast-changing church. Jesus was a Jew and he addressed his message in categories that spoke to the Palestinian Judaism of the first century. What was most on the minds of his contemporaries was the effort to define what it meant to be the people of God in the face of Roman domination. Closely allied to that effort was a debate over their understanding of God, the values that defined the Jewish people, and the way of life that grew out of those values.

Luke and his audience lived in a complicated world and a fast-changing church.

For Jews of every stripe, the distinction between religious and political commitments would have been meaningless. The nation was religious and religion was national in its scope. As a result, Roman conquest and domination of Palestine represented far more than a loss of political sovereignty. It represented a crisis of faith. What did it mean to be the people of God if the nation could not fulfill the destiny assigned to it? More basic yet was the question: if the nation cannot fulfill its destiny, how is God's sovereignty manifested and his promises fulfilled?

Broadly speaking, people answered those questions in one of two ways. The Zealots answered both questions in terms of rigorous obedience to the law that could only be achieved through independence from their Roman overlords. For the Zealots, or *Sicarii* as they were called, that independence was both the prerequisite for fulfilling

For Jesus and his contemporaries the basic question was: if the nation cannot fulfill its destiny, how is God's sovereignty manifested and his promises fulfilled?

their destiny and the visible expression of God's sovereignty. The Pharisees, or *Perishaya*, were equally committed to a strict observance of Jewish law (and in particular, levitical law). But if the *Sicarii*, or "dagger-carriers," favored revolt and thought of God as a warrior-king, the *Perishaya*, or "the separated ones," favored an observance of the law that achieved Israel's destiny by distinguishing its way of life from its neighbors and thought of God as separate or holy.

It was into this debate that Jesus entered and offered an equally complex response. He refused to give into Rome. He distinguished between devotion to God and devotion to the Empire, and he observed the law. Yet, at the same time, he also refused to participate wholeheartedly in one camp or the other, placing himself squarely in a crossfire between the two. He used the language of kingdom, but refused to think of God as a warrior-king. He worshipped in the Temple and studied the law, but he refused to

Broadly speaking, people answered those questions in one of two ways.

11

observe it in ways that put the pursuit of holiness above the expression of mercy or excluded taxpayers and sinners from the gracious embrace of God.

It was into this debate that Jesus entered and offered an equally complex response.

For all his differences with his contemporaries, however, it would be a mistake to think of Jesus in contemporary categories. He was not focused on "inclusion," nor did he think in terms of individual rights and liberties. His was not an interfaith or ecumenical enterprise; and he did not entertain political and nationalistic ideas that we would label political unless they were inextricably related to the question of how Israel could continue to be the people of God.

Gentiles represented the responsibility of Israel to be a blessing to the world and the focus of a mission that could only be realized after the nation first understood the nature of her destiny and her God.

Gentiles figured, of course, in his message and ministry. Because they did, Jesus provoked both the Zealots and Pharisees who found it hard to know how an emphasis upon the mercy shown toward Gentiles could be accommodated by an emphasis upon the strict of observance of the law and freedom from the Romans. It could even be reasonably argued that this feature of the teaching of Jesus gave the fledgling church (which was different from the Jewish sect that Jesus led) its missionary passion and its theological warrant for spreading the gospel "to the ends of the earth."

But Gentiles were peripheral to his message and to the issues that the preaching of Jesus raised. Far from being the focus of his message, Gentiles represented the responsibility of Israel to be a blessing to the world and the focus of a mission that could only be realized after the nation first understood the nature of her destiny and her God. When, in the face of Israel's failure to heed the coming of the kingdom, Gentiles began to enter the kingdom of God, they did so—according to Jesus—as a sign of judgment on the house of Israel. The old proverb we hear is "Beware of Greeks *bearing* gifts." But Jesus would have observed, "Beware of Greeks *receiving* gifts." When they do, the judgment of God is upon you.

"Beware of Greeks receiving gifts." When they do, the judgment of God is upon you.

This was inevitable. At its most fundamental, the people of Israel believed the world held only two kinds of people. One was Jewish. The other—the Greek or Gentile world—was not. Issues of racial, political, and social identity were not just secondary. They were irrelevant. Israel was not just at the heart of the story of her relationship with God. Israel was at the heart of God's story.

In fact, it could be argued that Gentiles were something of a plot complication in that story. They were, more often than not, the enemy—neighboring kingdoms and conquerors. Their chariots and religion were a source of temptation to Israel and a test of her faith. From time to time, they were the instruments of God's judgment, which was more jarring still. Even when Israel began to grapple with the universality of its message, Gentiles occupied a remote and problematic place in the debate. The story of Jonah, for example, affirms the responsibility of Israel to that other world, but it hardly provides a sympathetic portrait of Gentiles or even moves them to the center of God's story.

> *Gentiles were something of a plot complication in the story of redemption. That made storytelling in the early church a challenge.*

It is more than a little surprising, then, that the teaching of Jesus provided the precedent for the emerging church's ministry to Gentiles at all. But that is also why as a Jewish sect, early Christianity was ill-prepared to deal with the enthusiastic response of Gentiles to the teaching of the gospel, never mind their far greater numbers. Gentiles had a dubious and disputed place in the story that Israel typically told and yet—there they were. That made storytelling in the early church a challenge.

When Storytelling Gets Serious

Writers of fiction can find the plot of story difficult to orchestrate. Stories pass through twists and turns to a climactic turning point in the narrative, and typically what follows is what the French call the *denouement*, an unwinding of the plot. But this broad outline of what typically happens in a story hardly makes an author's task easier.

> *Plot complication poses one kind of challenge in fiction.*

There is still a delicate balance to be struck in telling the story. The closing chapters of the story cannot introduce utterly new elements, or foreclose on the narrative and begin another storyline. If that happens, an author can confuse the readers or lose them entirely.

Some writers have experimented with that balance. The short story writer O. Henry was famous for plots that included a surprise ending, and he was exceptionally effective at introducing new and unanticipated elements to a story that seemed to be ending in one way and actually ended in an entirely different fashion. But it is also possible to strain the fabric of a story to the extent that it is ruptured. When that happens writers are rightly accused of having failed to choose the story that they wanted to tell.

In religious storytelling the consequences are far more serious.

In religious storytelling, of course, the consequences are far more serious. As in spiritual direction and good therapy, a religious story has to hang together, no matter how deeply marked it might be by surprising or unanticipated endings. The ability of people to place themselves in the story and to trust the integrity of the account is intertwined with defining issues that go well beyond entertainment value. It touches on issues of

- Belonging
- Tradition
- Authority
- Behavior
- Hope

Tell a convincing story and all five of these elements of the spiritual life can be nourished and strengthened. An individual or a group of people can find a sense of kinship or belonging with God and others; they can grow to trust the reassurances that they have been given by God; they can begin to live out of a vocabulary and experience that gives shape to their lives; they can discover guidance for the way in which they live; and they can hope, which is something every community requires no matter how rich its spiritual and moral life.

The ability of people to place themselves in the story touches on issues of belonging, tradition, authority, behavior, and hope.

Tell a story that lacks coherence or persuasive power and all five elements can be compromised. People drift; they seek a different way of telling their story and they cultivate a different means of belonging, defining the authorities for their lives, a tradition out of which to live, a code by which to make moral choices, and another source of hope. Needs of that kind do not go away. If one story doesn't satisfy those needs, then another one is told.

For example, my friend Bill embraced the Episcopal Church, its liturgy and tradition, precisely because of the demands that it made upon his life and the meaning it offered him in exchange. Referring to himself (half-jokingly) as a "medieval Christian," he grew up in an amorphous spiritual tradition without grounding or content.

It served him well when he was young—or so he thought. It left him free to make choices without the constraints of belonging to a religious community. He could claim to be grounded spiritually when it suited him or made others comfortable. But his tour of duty in Vietnam, the death of his son, and his own subsequent health problems outstripped the resources of his commitments. In the years since, he has learned that belonging to a spiritual family is much like belonging to any family. Now eighty years old, he observes, "It may have sharp edges that make being a part of the family difficult. But the moral and spiritual grounding that belonging affords outweighs the occasional family tiff."

The Gentile Ending to a Jewish Story

In important ways Gentiles were a surprise ending to the story Palestinian Judaism told, akin to the endings that one might find in an O. Henry short story—a new and unanticipated chapter to an old, old story. In still other ways Gentiles constituted an entirely new story.

Gentiles were a surprise ending to the story Palestinian Judaism told.

If, of course, the influx of Gentiles into the early movement had simply represented a new kind of plot complication, it would have mattered very little. But the Gentile response to the gospel represented the same kind of delicate challenge to the earlier church's story that introducing a surprise ending poses for storytellers—with far higher stakes.

Continuity was essential to telling the story in a fashion that preserved the gifts of divine redemption and community that were inherent in Luke's gospel. Tell that story well and there were reasons for Gentiles to consider themselves a part of that ancient story and warrants for Jewish followers of Jesus to believe that their own journey was consistent with the faith that nurtured them and that Gentiles

Tell that story well and there were reasons for Gentiles to consider themselves a part of that ancient story.

belonged to that story as well. Tell the story in a way that the influx of Gentiles represented a rupture with the past and both gifts would have been lost to the fledgling Christian community.

This was the challenge that Luke faced. It is unlikely that he would have articulated it in this fashion, but it was the challenge to which he intuitively responded. Using the rhetorical skills of a man schooled in the Greco-Roman tradition, but steeped in the ancient and Jewish study of Scripture, he crafted a story that was unique among the literature preserved from the period. But it undoubtedly represented the crystallization of one of the dominant ways in which the sweeping story of the early church was being told. Its place in the New Testament canon, the lectionary, and the liturgy of the church certainly points to its persuasive power and its ability to shape the Christian story.

Luke told a story that reported what had happened, what was happening, and suggested something about what was about to happen. But his story was more than just a report, it helped to shape the self-understanding of the church and its future.

In that sense, Luke told a story that reported what had happened, what was happening, and suggested something about what was about to happen. But his story was more than just a report. As we will see, it helped to shape the self-understanding of the church and its future.

God's Story, the Church's Story, Our Story

What does this conversation about Luke's gospel say of abiding significance for the contemporary reader?

There is a great deal of storytelling done today. It takes many forms and it is told in many ways. Written and oral storytelling are still very common, but they are told using a variety of media. Indeed, given the nature of modern life, it can be reasonably argued that we are exposed to far more stories than were people who lived in the ancient world. That said, it is not clear that we rely as deeply on storytelling as did ancient cultures, nor do we own them as our own—or if we do, it is not clear that we are willing to admit it. Yet the practice of using stories is a part of our national heritage. Take for example the powerful way in which Abraham Lincoln in the Gettysburg Address briefly framed our national history, the place of the Civil

War in that history, and the significance of the federal government in the space of 272 words. The story implied in the opening sentence did most of the work: "Fourscore and seven years ago our fathers brought forth on this continent a new nation, conceived in liberty and dedicated to the proposition that all men are created equal."[11]

Luke's response to the challenges faced by the early church reminds us of the power of stories to give us our spiritual bearings, to engage us in meaningful conversations about the past, present, and future. It also reminds us of the power of those stories to shape both the individual and communal sense of who we are.

Luke's response to the challenges faced by the early church reminds us of the power of stories to give us our spiritual bearings, to engage us in meaningful conversations about the past, present, and future. It also reminds us of the power of those stories to shape both the individual and communal sense of who we are.

To believe that Luke's gospel had the power to encourage the kind of spiritual and communal formation described above is to say something about its power to continue making that kind of contribution to our own lives. As I said above, it is also a vital part of our claims for Luke's gospel as Scripture—in characterizing it as both inspired and revelatory.

But Scripture does not impose itself on our lives. It needs to be invited into a conversation with them, and it is only in seeing our lives as organically related to its story—as a chapter or a subplot in that larger story—that it can begin to touch us in ways that are inspired and revelatory. It is that ancient invitation that Luke's gospel continues to make.

CHAPTER TWO

Belonging

One of our oldest and most deeply rooted impulses, now often overlooked in our fast-paced culture, is the spiritual need to belong. In fact, there are those who suggest that we live in a spiritual world in which belonging no longer really matters to us—notwithstanding the social networks that people are so busily building via the Internet and text messages. But in a religious community there is no belonging that matters more than belonging to God. It grounds and defines every other kind of belonging.

> *One of our oldest and most deeply rooted impulses, now often overlooked in our fast-paced culture, is the spiritual need to belong.*

The Enduring Importance of Belonging

Charting the last half century of spiritual life in the United States, for example, sociologist Robert Wuthnow argues that we have turned from a spirituality of *dwelling* to a spirituality of *seeking* as our dominant mode of being in the world. Documenting the impact of massive immigration to the United States, the aspirations of GIs returning to their homes after World War II and the comparative prosperity of the 1950s, Wuthnow notes that Americans largely identified building and living in their homes with not only personal progress, but with spiritual progress as well. To be spiritual was to be at home in one's church, to attend regularly, to participate in its activities, even to help out in its construction and maintenance.

That spirituality of dwelling, Wuthnow argues, was deeply undermined by the turmoil of the 1960s. The war in Vietnam, racial tensions, and the Watergate incident not only undermined our confidence in the virtues of our civic institutions, they also helped to spread a malaise that raised serious doubts about the inherent virtue of our spiritual dwellings as well. Growing out of that disenchantment, he notes, Americans turned (or returned, some would argue with good reason) to a spirituality that emphasized seeking instead of dwelling and rootedness.[12]

Interestingly, we may be already witnessing a reaction to that trend as American baby boomers age and their influence begins to wane. Their children, who are influenced by more than one generational dynamic, are already turning to forms of spiritual expression and community that emphasize—albeit in new ways—the virtues of rootedness and belonging that characterized the lives of their grandparents. Notably, the younger generation is also emphasizing the kind of belonging that stresses not just the community where they live in the here and now, but a sense of belonging to a community with a story deeply rooted in the past.

Generational patterns of this kind are interesting, but they are not particularly instructive or significant in and of themselves. What is of greater significance is the pendulum-like swing between the generations and the spiritual values that surface and resurface over much longer periods of time.

There is a kind of generational conceit that believes a given era has made discoveries that no other generation has ever made. In technological and scientific arenas there is a case to be made for some of those claims. A generation can break that kind of new ground and there are many historical examples to which one can point.

Spiritual needs have a universal and perennial character that reassert themselves in spite of the claims that any one generation may make.

But spiritual needs have a universal and perennial character that reassert themselves in spite of the claims that any one generation may make. So while one generation may value seeking over belonging, that does not mean that a sense of spiritual belonging has become somehow obsolete. In fact, the tendency to rediscover the need to belong suggests a completely different possibility. Perhaps spiritual belonging nurtures the kind of security that makes seeking possible, while seeking is by definition the search for a new sense of belonging.

Some would go even further and argue that the emphasis on seeking that so dominated the closing decades of the twentieth century had very little to do with spiritual impulses at all, but were the product of a generation educated and trained to value questions and doubt certainty of any kind. Noting that university faculties were often dedicated to thorough-going skepticism about the possibility of knowing anything religious, they observe that the emphasis on seeking became a means of inculcating a spirituality that was shaped by the same fundamental skepticism about knowing God.

Be that as it may, it remains true that the need for spiritual belonging never goes away. Indeed, students of comparative religion argue that belonging is the essence of religious belief. To hold something to be true religiously is to assert that God exists, to confess a connection with God, and to belong to a world ordered by God.

The need for spiritual belonging never goes away.

To belong in this way holds at bay a sense of being lost or alone. It orders our perceptions of the world around us and it connects us with a community of other believers. As such, it nurtures a sense of belonging not only to God and to the world, but to other human beings. This is why even avowedly unreligious (and even antireligious) people end up belonging to something that is defining for them and gives them that sense of belonging, be it a philosophy of life, private spirituality, or political movement.

Belonging Lost

It is this primal human need both to seek and to belong that provides an entry point into the Gentile world of Luke's gospel. A sense of belonging to God was never easy to achieve for the Gentiles of Luke's church. Scattered across the Mediterranean, Gentiles who were drawn to the Jewish faith and to what we would now call emerging Christianity found themselves suspended between two worlds.

A sense of belonging to God was never easy to achieve for the Gentiles of Luke's church.

The world out of which they came was polytheistic and syncretistic. That is, they worshipped multiple gods and freely combined religious beliefs. From a modern and monotheistic point of view, it is easy to characterize their religious world as chaotic or to simply label it "pagan." But it is more accurate and helpful in describing the predicament of Gentile Christians to describe it as "complex." It was also dramatically changed by the fortunes of the empire itself.

The earliest belief system could be described as *agrarian* or *agricultural* in its orientation. Roman beliefs as forged on the Italian peninsula had initially grown out of the early religious practice in farming communities. The gods to whom people prayed were known by the task that they performed, rather than by their virtues or character. In that regard, their roles were sharply refined, some charged with the care of the hearth, others the threshold—still others, the hinges on the doors of a home.

The sense of belonging that the average Roman experienced could hardly be described as "organized religion," and it is not clear that these beliefs were widely shared from village to village. But it was not the personal or private faith of modern individualism. Shared by families and, perhaps, within villages, such religion was closely tied to home and hearth. As such, their sense of spiritual belonging derived from familial associations with their worship, as well as the place of their gods in the rigors and routines of daily life. Prayers, for that reason, were typically for protection and provision of basic needs.

As Rome grew in power and spread its control by conquest, the religious picture began to change as well. During this period of *early colonization*, at first Romans "invoked" the gods who were worshiped by the people they conquered. Building temples to the more prominent ones, they invited those gods to become gods of Rome, and there is even evidence to suggest that they sometimes embraced new cults associated with those gods. As such, it could be argued that a new layer of "belonging" was added to the hearth-based and agrarian experience of early Romans.

But it is easy to overestimate the significance of those changes; and it would be a mistake to suggest that the changes were universal. The practice of appropriating the gods of other peoples as gods of Rome was not a practice that lasted long. Vortumnus, the god of orchards and fruit, was the last god to be invoked in this fashion in 246 BCE. Furthermore, evidence suggests that Romans continued to worship their own homegrown gods. It is more accurate, then, to argue that for *some* Romans a new kind of religious belonging began to emerge. It is also likely that this new kind of belonging was more common in urban centers, where the first converts to Christianity lived.

By the time Rome became a true empire and entered the *imperial period*, the cultural climate had changed again. Romans were more confident of their own cultural ascendancy. As a result, they were also more certain of their own religious practice and more tolerant of religious practice elsewhere in the empire. In some cases the gods of other religions were given new names and assimilated into the Roman pantheon of gods. So, for example, Jupiter the king of gods, was renamed Zeus, and Ares, the god of war, became Mars. Elsewhere religious practice native to the region flourished alongside Roman worship.

During the imperial period, the Romans also began to assign divine attributes to their emperors as well. This system of worship overlaid the existing religious practice of the Empire, adding an element of political loyalty to issues of religious belonging and fidelity.

This is not to say that Romans were tolerant of every kind of religious practice or that they were uniform in their attitudes. They were particularly opposed to human sacrifice and, as a result, they actively suppressed some religious sects in North Africa, Gaul, Spain, and Britain that practiced it. There is also little doubt that some Romans rejected one or more religious practices out of hand.[13]

It was this world that Luke's Gentile converts to Christianity inhabited. But even this brief description illustrates how difficult it is to talk about *the* Gentile experience. It cannot be assumed—as it so often is—that all Gentiles believed in and combined the same religious influences that were in play in their world. Social, physical, and economic factors—as well as a hundred and one far more

It is difficult to talk about the Gentile experience, but in general embracing the Christian faith would have deeply compromised Gentiles' sense of belonging in their families, villages or towns, and ethnic groups that still practiced polytheism, worshipping numerous gods.

personal considerations—no doubt contributed to kaleidoscopic variety. So just which of these complex forces any individual embraced and how deeply they embraced them is an open question. In general, this can be said:

- The singular commitments associated with the Christian faith would have represented a substantial break with the religious ethos in which the typical Gentile was reared. To say "I believe in one God" to the exclusion of all others would have put the average Christian in a very small minority, shared only by the Jews who worshipped in synagogues scattered across the Mediterranean.
- For that reason, the commitments of Gentile converts to Christianity would have struck their neighbors as exclusive, extreme, and unnecessary.
- As a consequence, embracing the Christian faith would have deeply compromised Gentiles' sense of belonging in their families, villages or towns, and ethnic groups that still practiced polytheism, worshipping numerous gods.

Belonging Postponed

But matters for the Gentiles who were drawn to the fledgling Christian faith were more complicated still. If they had felt that they had left one world behind them, it was equally difficult to feel a sense of belonging in the new religious world into which they had moved.

> If Gentiles felt that they had left one world behind them, it was equally difficult to feel a sense of belonging in the new religious world into which they had moved.

What we describe today as Christianity was, at first, a sect within Judaism and only over time did it acquire a sense of its own, separate identity. So to become a Christian was not just a matter of finding a sense of belonging in one religion, but effectively in two. Early Jewish-Christians were just as unclear and divided on how Jewish you needed to be to be a Christian, as Gentiles were unclear what was expected of them. As a result, heated debates persisted over the place of circumcision and the importance of dietary laws, as we read in Acts 15:1ff.

This was not a simple matter of gatekeeping on the part of Christianity's Jewish adherents. Judaism was also an embattled sect. Its own monotheistic commitments made it extremely demanding of its followers, and it had already suffered for millennia with cycles of war, defeat, foreign domination, and exile. By the time that Jesus was born, Israel was deeply under the control of its Roman overlords, and by the time that Luke wrote his gospel, Jerusalem had been sacked and the Temple destroyed.

To become a Christian was not just a matter of finding a sense of belonging in one religion, but effectively in two.

Understandably, then, Jews were trying to strengthen their faith so that they would be immune to foreign interference. They had already done this during the Babylonian exile (597/586–538 BCE) when they were forced from their homeland, and again during the reign of Antichus IV Epiphanes (175–164 BCE) when they lived under the control of their Greek conquerors. That is why the court heroes mentioned in the book of Daniel—Daniel, Shadrach, Mechach, and Abednego—are described as having kept the law of God, in spite of pagan influence and demands (Dan 1–6), and why the heroes of the stories were hailed as defenders of the true faith.

The Pharisees took this quest a significant step further by nurturing the kingdom within, advocating thorough-going adherence to the law that reflected an inner dedication to the God of Israel.[14] They were convinced that the vitality of the Jewish faith depended upon developing a spirituality that lay beyond the ability of foreign powers to conquer Israel or destroy the Temple. So instead they promoted an observance of oral religious law that elaborated on the Torah and brought the whole of life under God's dominion. This "hidden revolution" in Jewish life, as one scholar describes it, not only shaped the practice of their faith in their own day, but lived on as what is often described today as rabbinic Judaism.[15] The Pharisees' approach to the Jewish faith decisively shaped the future of Judaism in the late second century CE and eventually insured the survival of Judaism in spite of centuries of anti-Semitism.

The Pharisees nurtured "the kingdom within," advocating thorough-going adherence to the law that reflected an inner dedication to the God of Israel.

While it is unlikely that many Jewish Christians in Luke's day were Pharisees, there is little doubt that their observance of the Jewish faith had been significantly shaped by this millennia-long quest

25

While it is unlikely that many Jewish Christians in Luke's day were Pharisees, there is little doubt that their observance of the Jewish faith had been significantly shaped by their quest to be faithful. It is not surprising that when Gentiles became a part of the fledgling church in ever greater numbers, their attitudes toward circumcision, food laws, and other Jewish practices were as much at issue as was their faith in Jesus.

to be faithful. So it is not surprising that when Gentiles became a part of the fledgling church in ever greater numbers, their attitudes toward circumcision, food laws, and other Jewish practices were as much at issue as was their faith in Jesus (Acts 15; Gal 2).

Exactly how individual Gentiles navigated the experience of being suspended between two worlds without belonging fully to either one no doubt varied a great deal. Here are some general observations:

- For God-fearers who lived in the shadow of the synagogue and embraced Judaism to one degree or another, the debates over their relationship to the fledgling church might have seemed inevitable. But if they had not fully committed to Judaism—and many of them had not—the controversy must have forced them to confront their ambivalence about both the faith to which they had been drawn and the faith they were now embracing.
- For those who converted directly to Christianity, the demands made by Jewish Christians posed a different set of challenges. They had already moved away from their native practice, but now they were being told that in a sense they needed to become observant Jews before they could become Christians.
- For both groups of Gentiles, there was still another problem. Although the teaching of Jesus had its origins in Judaism, relatively few Jews had responded to the gospel. The legitimacy both of the faith that they were embracing and the legitimacy of their place in it were, no doubt, a source of anxiety to Gentile Christians of every stripe.

God-fearer: An umbrella term describing Gentiles who were deeply committed to Jewish theology and practice but were unwilling or unable to undergo circumcision to become Jews.

- The families of Gentile Christians often ostracized those members who converted. (Even polytheists have their limits.) There was a personal and social price to be paid for abandoning the faith of one's extended family networks.

Telling a Story of Belonging

Luke, in response to the issues confusing both Jewish and Gentile Christians, crafts his gospel as a story of belonging. Because his medium is a story, he cannot make the kind of sustained and more obvious argument he might make in an epistle. But he weaves many of the same points he might have made by crafting the drama that he is about to unfold. Gentiles figure in the narrative at a number of points throughout the gospel, but there are four vignettes in which they play a strategic role:

- The prologue to the gospel (Luke 1:1–4)
- The inaugural prophecy (Luke 2:29–35)
- The inaugural sermon (Luke 4:16–30)
- The inaugural ministry (Luke 10:1–20)

Luke, in response to the issues confusing both Jewish and Gentile Christians, crafts his gospel as a story of belonging.

Using these four passages, Luke:

- Draws his readers into the story
- Positions them in the saving history that is the work of God in Christ
- Accounts for the cool response of Israel to Jesus
- Validates their own presence in the church

The Prologue to the Gospel (Luke 1:1–4)

Luke begins by placing his hearers front and center in the story:

> Since many have undertaken to set down an orderly account of the events that have been fulfilled among us, just as they were handed on to us by those who from the beginning were eyewitnesses and servants of the word, I too decided, after investigating everything carefully from the very first, to write an orderly account for you, most excellent Theophilus, so that you may know the truth concerning the things about which you have been instructed. (Luke 1:1–4)

By addressing his gospel using the literary device "most excellent Theophilus," Luke is not being clever. By using it, he places his Gentile listeners on the front row of the storytelling he is about to do. By calling them "lovers of God" who have been "instructed," he also asserts—at the outset—their

Luke begins by placing his hearers front and center in the story calling them "lovers of God."

spiritual belonging. They have a connection with God and they have been initiated into the story that Luke is about to tell.

The connection with God is, of course, of preeminent importance. Belonging to a community of believers can be reassuring, but in a religious community there is no belonging more important than belonging to God. It anchors and insures every other kind of belonging possible. It trumps all protests to the contrary, and it no doubt reassured Gentile Christians who had good reason to believe that not every member of the community thought they belonged.

But Luke also asserts that they belong to the story he is about to tell. They are not just auditors. They have already been "instructed"—the Greek says "catechized"—in the things that they are about to hear, foreshadowing the approach which the church would eventually use to introduce new believers to the faith.

For much the same reason, he repeatedly uses the first person plural in the first few verses. The events Luke describes "have been fulfilled among *us*, just as they were handed on to *us* by those who from the beginning were eyewitnesses and servants of the word." They belong, in other words, not just to God, not just to the faith in which they have been instructed, but to the larger story of God's saving work in Christ that he is about to describe. Hence Luke uses the language of beginning, fulfillment, and the reference to "the word," which probably refers to Jesus and his teaching.

The way in which a story of this kind begins can make all the difference to the way in which those who hear it connect with it. If the story is told in the third person ("he, she, they") and the events described are things that transpired in another place, time, and community, then we might not connect with the story at all. It might be interesting and even entertaining, but we don't necessarily consider ourselves a part of the events. It's a bit like reading a high school history book.

The story Luke tells is more like a family album than a history book.

Luke's introduction does exactly the opposite. It's more like a family album than a high school history book. The story is his church's story, the people described are their spiritual relatives, and the God orchestrating it all is the one in who finally governs the outcome. The introduction makes that immediately clear.

An Inaugural Prophecy (Luke 2:29–35)

Of course, like the best of genuinely healthy spiritual stories, it's not all about us; and Luke's story is not all about Gentiles. But he does work quickly to anchor the Gentile experience in the specifics of the biblical story and salvation history. His first effort appears early in the story of Jesus.

He describes the circumstances of Jesus' birth in terms a Gentile audience would have associated with a miraculous event, but he uses language that any Jewish reader would have connected with the stories from Jewish scriptures. Then, shortly after his birth, Joseph and Mary present Jesus at the Temple.

Luke's story is not all about Gentiles. He work quickly to anchor the Gentile experience in the specifics of the biblical story and salvation history.

Simeon is present. We know only what Luke tells us about him, though tradition has tried to fill in the blanks. He is "righteous and devout." He has been "looking forward to the consolation of Israel," and God has promised that he will see the Messiah before he dies.

In response to the presentation of Jesus in the Temple, he takes the baby in his arms and speaks at the prompting of the Spirit:

> "Master, now you are dismissing your servant in peace, according to your word; for my eyes have seen your salvation, which you have prepared in the presence of all peoples, a light for revelation to the Gentiles and for glory to your people Israel." (Luke 2:29–32)

Registering the surprise of Joseph and Mary, Simeon blesses them and then tells Mary:

> "This child is destined for the falling and the rising of many in Israel, and to be a sign that will be opposed so that the inner thoughts of many will be revealed—and a sword will pierce your own soul too." (Luke 2:34b–35)

It is easy and perhaps natural to be caught up in the personal dimensions of what the old man has to say about Mary's fate. But that is neither the central point of the story, nor is it likely to be what caught the attention of Luke's hearers. Reading the story with the focus on Mary is a way of reading it *after* Christianity is securely established.

Instead, our focus should be on Simeon, a man with impeccable Jewish credentials. He is a student of Israel's history and, more significantly, Israel's place in the saving work of God. Mary and Joseph have brought Jesus to the Temple—which is the institution that lies at the heart of all it means to be a child of God—and their intention is to fulfill the law. All of this sets the scene. Simeon is an independent and credible witness. Mary and Joseph are observant Jews. The ritual is precisely what observant Jews would do.

Simeon is an independent and credible Jewish witness. Mary and Joseph are observant Jews. The ritual is precisely what observant Jews would do.

Then, with Jesus in his arms, Simeon—this credible, faithful servant who watches and waits for the Lord's Messiah—defines how Jesus will fulfill this long-held hope:

- He is, first and foremost, "a light for revelation to the Gentiles" and "for glory" (a revelation of God's presence and splendor) to the people of Israel (v. 32).
- His preaching will bring with it both judgment, "the falling," and salvation, "the rising," of many in Israel (v. 34).

The words of Simeon affirm the Gentiles' struggle to belong in the prophetic heritage of Judaism and they explain the limited number of Jewish converts.

It isn't what anyone expected. But for Gentiles, who wonder if they belong and why so few Jews have responded to a Jewish message, Simeon's words are reassuring. They affirm the Gentiles' struggle to belong in the prophetic heritage of Judaism and they explain the limited number of Jewish converts.

An Inaugural Sermon (Luke 4:16–30)

In what might be described as Jesus' inaugural sermon in Nazareth, Luke wastes no time in expanding on this theme:

> When he came to Nazareth, where he had been brought up, he went to the synagogue on the sabbath day, as was his custom. He stood up to read, and the scroll of the prophet Isaiah was given to him. He unrolled the scroll and found the place where it was written:
>
>> "The Spirit of the Lord is upon me,
>> because he has anointed me
>> to bring good news to the poor.

He has sent me to proclaim release to the captives
and recovery of sight to the blind,
to let the oppressed go free,
to proclaim the year of the Lord's favour."

In what might be described as Jesus' inaugural sermon in Nazareth, Luke wastes no time in expanding on this theme.

And he rolled up the scroll, gave it back to the attendant, and sat down. The eyes of all in the synagogue were fixed on him. Then he began to say to them, "Today this scripture has been fulfilled in your hearing." All spoke well of him and were amazed at the gracious words that came from his mouth. They said, "Is not this Joseph's son?" He said to them, "Doubtless you will quote to me this proverb, 'Doctor, cure yourself!' And you will say, 'Do here also in your home town the things that we have heard you did at Capernaum.'" And he said, "Truly I tell you, no prophet is accepted in the prophet's home town. But the truth is, there were many widows in Israel in the time of Elijah, when the heaven was shut up for three years and six months, and there was a severe famine over all the land; yet Elijah was sent to none of them except to a widow at Zarephath in Sidon. There were also many lepers in Israel in the time of the prophet Elisha, and none of them was cleansed except Naaman the Syrian." When they heard this, all in the synagogue were filled with rage. They got up, drove him out of the town, and led him to the brow of the hill on which their town was built, so that they might hurl him off the cliff. But he passed through the midst of them and went on his way. (Luke 4:16–30)

To us, Luke's description of this situation may sound a bit like a history lesson or a story just about the ministry of Jesus. But to his dominantly Gentile church—which was locked in the painful struggles associated with having left one spiritual home and trying to belong to another—it was anything but a matter of history. The major elements in his description of this sermon and confrontation in Nazareth sets out not just the tensions that existed in Jesus' own day, but in Luke's church as well.

To us, Luke's description of this situation may sound a bit like a history lesson or a story just about the ministry of Jesus. But to his dominantly Gentile church— which was locked in the painful struggles associated with having left one spiritual home and trying to belong to another—it was anything but a matter of history.

One element is the open affirmation of the Jewishness of both Jesus and his message. He may be a Galilean, and Galileans were reputedly far less rigorous in their observance of the law. But here he is in the synagogue reading from the prophecy of Isaiah (Isa 61:1; 58:6; 61:2) and plainly declaring his own ministry as a fulfillment of the prophet's expectations. He even uses the word "anointed" to describe his mission and, therefore, his messianic credentials.

But the congregation is not impressed for very long. He no sooner identifies his message with things Jewish, than he names the resistance that he anticipates. Even more pointedly he identifies their resistance to his message with the times in Jewish history that the nation had refused to listen. When they did, Jesus notes, God sent messengers and healing to Gentiles instead:

> "But the truth is, there were many widows in Israel in the time of Elijah, when the heaven was shut up for three years and six months, and there was a severe famine over all the land; yet Elijah was sent to none of them except to a widow at Zarephath in Sidon. There were also many lepers in Israel in the time of the prophet Elisha, and none of them was cleansed except Naaman the Syrian." (Luke 4:25–27)

In putting this inaugural sermon (we could say, inaugural confrontation) where he does, Luke has introduced the ancient and Jewish roots of the message that Jesus taught. He has again accounted for the modest response that he received from the Jewish community and, by inference, the modest response that the church has had to the proclamation of the gospel. In the same brief space, he has also identified the precedent that was set long ago for the salvation of the Gentiles: God's grace moves where it finds need and a receptive spirit (1 Kgs 17:1–16; 2 Kgs 5:1–14).

Luke has identified the precedent that was set long ago for the salvation of the Gentiles: God's grace moves where it finds need and a receptive spirit.

An Inaugural Ministry (Luke 10:1–20)

Finally, Luke draws his Gentile listeners even more deeply into the story of the Christian community by recounting the mission of the seventy. Unique to his gospel, this story recounts the sending of seventy of Jesus' disciples out in pairs to preach and heal:

> After this the Lord appointed seventy others and sent them on ahead of him in pairs to every town and place where he himself intended to go. He said to them, "The harvest is plentiful, but the labourers are few; therefore ask the Lord of the harvest to send out labourers into his har-

vest. Go on your way. See, I am sending you out like lambs into the midst of wolves. Carry no purse, no bag, no sandals; and greet no one on the road. Whatever house you enter, first say, 'Peace to this house!' And if anyone is there who shares in peace, your peace will rest on that person; but if not, it will return to you. Remain in the same house, eating and drinking whatever they provide, for the labourer deserves to be paid. Do not move about from house to house. Whenever you enter a town and its people welcome you, eat what is set before you; cure the sick who are there, and say to them, 'The kingdom of God has come near to you.' But whenever you enter a town and they do not welcome you, go out into its streets and say, 'Even the dust of your town that clings to our feet, we wipe off in protest against you. Yet know this: the kingdom of God has come near.' I tell you, on that day it will be more tolerable for Sodom than for that town.

> *Luke draws his Gentile listeners even more deeply into the story of the Christian community by recounting the mission of the seventy.*

"Woe to you, Chorazin! Woe to you, Bethsaida! For if the deeds of power done in you had been done in Tyre and Sidon, they would have repented long ago, sitting in sackcloth and ashes. But at the judgement it will be more tolerable for Tyre and Sidon than for you.

And you, Capernaum,
will you be exalted to heaven?
No, you will be brought down to Hades.

"Whoever listens to you listens to me, and whoever rejects you rejects me, and whoever rejects me rejects the one who sent me."
The seventy returned with joy, saying, "Lord, in your name even the demons submit to us!" He said to them, "I watched Satan fall from heaven like a flash of lightning. See, I have given you authority to tread on snakes and scorpions, and over all the power of the enemy; and nothing will hurt you. Nevertheless, do not rejoice at this, that the spirits submit to you, but rejoice that your names are written in heaven."
(Luke 10:1–20)

Scholars disagree about the significance of the number seventy (and some Greek manuscripts read seventy-two). Essentially there are two positions that most scholars take. Some argue that seventy alludes to the number of Gentile nations referred to in a list found in the book of Genesis (Gen 10:2–31). These scholars believe that the number of emissaries sent out by Jesus was chosen to symbolize those nations and by inference, the church's mission to the Gentiles and the universality of the gospel.

Others hold that the number alludes to the seventy elders whom Moses selected to assist him in his responsibilities to the nation Israel, and who likewise were given the gift of prophecy (Num 11:16–17, 25). For these scholars, the key comparison being made is that of Jesus with Moses—as leader of the people of Israel and as prophet. They also argue that Luke would not have included a reference to Gentile mission this early in his two-part work, but would have saved a description of the Gentile mission for the book of Acts.

I am not convinced that Luke chose between the two possibilities or felt that he needed to choose. There is precedent in biblical literature and in ancient Jewish interpretation of Scripture to play with the possibilities, and the number seventy certainly works well that way here. Moses, as we will see, is an important point of comparison with Jesus for Luke. He is the first patriarch of the nation, its progenitor, the giver of the law, and a prophet par excellence.

But the allusions to the cities of Sodom, Tyre, and Sidon also make sense, if Luke has in mind the symbolic reference to the number of Gentile nations. Nor is a reference to a Gentile mission at this point in Luke-Acts necessarily out of place. There are three reasons a reference to Gentiles is appropriate here:

- A mission to Gentile and Samaritan cities in Palestine is not the same thing—nor is it of the same scale—as the mission we associate with Paul's ministry. No contemporary of Luke's would have confused this early mission of the seventy with that later and larger effort.

- The church's interest in Gentile mission is not likely to have been its own invention, but was grounded in Jesus' own ministry. So the fact that Jesus' own ministry parallels the ministry of the church is not particularly surprising—quite the reverse, actually.

- Finally, this mission was not just about a prophetic call to Gentiles, but was grounded in what Jesus believed to be a consequence of the coming of the kingdom. Again, it is a way of saying to a Jewish audience: "Beware of Greeks receiving (not bearing) gifts—when they do, the judgment is upon you."

The fact that Luke includes the story of the sending of the seventy further draws his Gentile audience into the drama that was the life and ministry of Jesus. They had already registered the role that Gentiles played in the inaugural prophecy and sermon that Luke had described. But now they could see the same explanation for their place in the church worked out in terms of a concrete mission in the context of Jesus' own ministry. This symbolic act of sending the seventy served as a precursor to the founding of their own churches and their baptism in the Christian faith. They belonged.

The symbolic act of sending the seventy served as a precursor to the founding of Gentile churches and their baptism in the Christian faith.

Belonging Then and Now

As we look for the possible connections between Luke's gospel and our own thinking about the tensions between belonging and seeking, it would be easy to assume that Luke's first audience struggled with some variation on the struggles we experience. But that would be to overlook the considerable differences between our context and the context of the gospel that we considered in chapter one.

The dialog between our world and Luke's is arguably one of emphasis. Nonetheless, I believe that these distinctions can be made:

It would be easy to assume that Luke's first audience struggled with some variation on the struggles we experience.

- Belonging then was communal and familial, and only secondarily an individual matter. Today we tend to belong as individuals, so it is hard to recognize the communal and familial aspects.
- Belonging was rarely considered optional. Religiously you had to belong somewhere. Today we tend to think of belonging as optional and we often craft a private spirituality.
- Belonging was defining for the early Christian community. Today belonging to a church—if it defines us at all—is one self-definition among many.

Cultures tend to have a voice, an emphasis, and an emotional and social center. In the United States that emotional and social center is the individual. We have other defining familial connections, friendships, associations, and memberships, but those take shape around our individual identity. We can, and often do, abandon all of those other relationships in the quest to be the best and happiest individual we can be. The necessity of such larger connections is often lost on us, even if, in fact, we are deeply dependent upon those connections.

By contrast, in the Greco-Roman world and in first-century Palestine, familial and communal connections defined the individual. The *pater familias*, the head of the household—usually the father—decided that the family would convert to a new religion, and individuals within the family—wives and children—followed as a matter of course.

The difference, however, is not just a matter of the means by which one becomes a part of this religion or that one. The commitment to a familial and communal self-understanding means that in some senses, the individual's identity depends finally upon those associations. To belong is to exist. To not belong is to cease to exist.

In ancient Rome, you did not even have a name. Parents numbered their male children and gave the feminine form of the father's name—without a number—to all of their daughters. So, for example, if Julius had three sons and two daughters, they were named Julius I, Julius II, Julius III, Julia, and Julia. So a disowned convert to the Christian faith was not only left without an inheritance, but without a name as well.

> The belonging that the Gentiles of Luke's church sought is fundamentally different from the kind of belonging that we often associate with membership in a church.

The belonging, then, that the Gentiles of Luke's church sought is fundamentally different from the kind of belonging that we often associate with membership in a church. For us the language of membership is associative and elective, it is not ontological—it does not define what we are at the core of our being. We belong to a church *and* a political party. We have a membership in the YMCA or the Elks.

For that reason, religious belonging tends to be optional for us (and that is no small problem of another kind). But for Luke's church, belonging was a necessity. You inevitably belonged somewhere. The only question that might arise was where. It is against that background that Luke's church would have heard the words of Jesus:

> "Do you think that I have come to bring peace to the earth? No, I tell you, but rather division! From now on, five in one household will be divided, three against two and two against three; they will be divided:
>
> father against son
> and son against father,
> mother against daughter
> and daughter against mother,
> mother-in-law against her daughter-in-law
> and daughter-in-law against mother-in-law." (Luke 12:51–59)

That is still the case in the Middle East today, which is why our approach to interfaith conversations is so puzzling to people from that part of the world. As Americans we can blithely talk about interfaith conversations that focus on what we all believe, regardless of our religious commitments. In our rush to be conciliatory, we fail to see that such constructs are, in the final analysis, something none of us believes. To talk about the "higher power" behind all religions, a commitment to "spirit," or the moral goodness in every religion begs for definition. What are the characteristics of the higher power to which we refer? What does that higher power value? What spirit? What kind of spirit? Are we talking about something more than simply the nonmaterial universe? What do we mean by moral goodness? Which values or actions are essential to the goodness we see in all religions? Why some values and not others?[16]

Religious belonging tends to be optional for us, but for Luke's church, belonging was a necessity.

But in the Middle East, as in Luke's world, the notion of a common denominator between religions would be incomprehensible. If you were part of a religion, you were part of a tribe, and along with that belonging came all the defining characteristics that made you who you were. The familial, religious, social, and national dimensions of life that we often sift and separate were part of an indistinguishable whole, and with it came identity, a way of life, sustenance, and support. If you were not part of a religious community, you ceased to exist. Belonging was not just desirable. It was a necessity.

The familial, religious, social, and national dimensions of life that we often sift and separate were part of an indistinguishable whole, and with it came identity, a way of life, sustenance, and support. If you were not part of a religious community, you ceased to exist.

In turn, belonging that is necessary is also defining. In a culture in which the individual is at the center of all that happens, religious belonging becomes one of many associations and, if it is defining at all, it is one of many self-definitions. I may be a Christian, but I am also Democrat or a Republican, a Georgian or a New Yorker, a Rotarian or a Mason. Some of those associations may matter more than others; some may not shape my life at all. But for the Christians of Luke's church, religious belonging was defining. If the monotheistic claims of their faith put them at odds with their Roman contemporaries, it was not because it put them at odds with other kinds of communal belonging—it was because the exclusive demands of Christianity, like the demands made by Judaism, made it impossible to connect with a Greco-Roman culture that could not comprehend a transcendent claim like that.

One of my colleagues used to tell his students the story of an early Christian whom had been imprisoned for his faith. The story, so it goes, was that the Roman authorities demanded to know, "Where are your people from?" The burden of the question was communal and ethnic. You knew a person's name and their identity on the basis of their tribal belonging. His only answer was, "*Ego Christus sum*—I am Christ's." The magistrate was livid and ordered his execution.

"Ego Christus sum—I am Christ's."

The story is often told as a tale of martyrdom, but it is, in fact, a story of identity. The prisoner was executed not because of what he believed, per se, but because of the way in which his beliefs placed him beyond official control. He could not be identified and managed by conventional Roman understandings of belonging. He belonged to Christ and the other categories did not matter.

CHAPTER THREE

Tradition

Unlike our own world in which traditions are easily jettisoned, Luke and his contemporaries inhabited traditions the way in which we might use a map or a global positioning system. Traditions helped you to find yourself in relationship to history, in relationship to the world around you, and even more importantly, in relationship to God.

Luke's preoccupation with things Gentile, along with the negative light in which he portrays the responses of Jews to the preaching of Jesus, might lead to the conclusion that Luke is either uninterested or hostile to Judaism. But nothing could be further from the truth. To be sure, the response of Israel to the teaching of Jesus was certainly a problem of theodicy for Luke and his church. If God is in control and the preaching of Jesus was God's message to Israel, then why did Jews respond in such small numbers?[17]

Traditions help you to find yourself in relationship to history, in relationship to world around you, and even more importantly, in relationship to God. In important ways the Jewish tradition was Luke's tradition.

But that doesn't mean that Luke was indifferent to Judaism or hostile to it. In fact, it could be reasonably argued that Luke addresses the issue because Jewish tradition was

Theodicy: Reconciling the notion that God is good and in control with events that seem to frustrate the purposes of God, including evil and unfulfilled promises.

in important ways, his tradition. Or to put it another way: problems of theodicy are only as real to you as the God who is having problems is real to you. If the God of Israel hadn't been very real to Luke, the response of Israel would not have been a problem either.

The God of Israel (as Luke's church understood God) was having a lot of problems. The message of Jesus had struck home with people who lived on the fringes of Israel's society. He had more success with people who were ritually unclean than with the religious elite who were fully observant in their practice of their faith. He spent more time with tax collectors and sinners than he did with leaders of the synagogue. And when he was crucified, even his closest followers abandoned him. If God was in this, why did Jesus' mission look like such a miserable failure?

At the time Luke wrote his gospel, it is hard to be sure about how large the church was, but the response to Jesus among Jews was clearly tepid. One scholar estimates that the church of Acts 1:14–15 had 120 members and by the fourth century it had between 5 and 7.5 million members.[18] As quickly as Christianity would grow among the nations, Luke was much closer in time to the church of 120 members and only a small fraction of that 120 were Jews.

If God was in this, why did Jesus' mission look like such a miserable failure?

So one question after another arose for Luke and other Gentile Christians:

- If Jesus was a Jew and preached a message relevant to Jews, then why had so few responded to him?
- If very few Jews responded positively to his message, what did that say about the validity of his message?
- Could it be that Jews failed to respond because they knew something about God and God's truth that Gentile Christians didn't understand?
- Even if the message was legitimate, how could they, as Gentiles, effectively carry the responsibility for the proclamation of the gospel?

As difficult as those questions were, there is little doubt that the distances, isolation, and small numbers in the early churches made those questions even more difficult to answer with any certainty.

In response, Luke could have jettisoned the Jewish past of Jesus, but instead he works from the tradition from the very start. The stories that help to shape that approach appear in the first three chapters of his gospel, at the end in chapter 24, and in key stories told in chapters 9 and 10. We will think about them together in that order.

Tradition: From the Beginning

Following the introductory verses to his gospel, Luke begins his story with the appearance of an angel to Zechariah announcing the birth of John the Baptist:

> Once when he was serving as priest before God and his section was on duty, he was chosen by lot, according to the custom of the priesthood, to enter the sanctuary of the Lord and offer incense. Now at the time of the incense-offering, the whole assembly of the people was praying outside. Then there appeared to him an angel of the Lord, standing at the right side of the altar of incense. When Zechariah saw him, he was terrified; and fear overwhelmed him. But the angel said to him, "Do not be afraid, Zechariah, for your prayer has been heard. Your wife Elizabeth will bear you a son, and you will name him John. You will have joy and gladness, and many will rejoice at his birth, for he will be great in the sight of the Lord. He must never drink wine or strong drink; even before his birth he will be filled with the Holy Spirit. He will turn many of the people of Israel to the Lord their God. With the spirit and power of Elijah he will go before him, to turn the hearts of parents to their children, and the disobedient to the wisdom of the righteous, to make ready a people prepared for the Lord." Zechariah said to the angel, "How will I know that this is so? For I am an old man, and my wife is getting on in years." The angel replied, "I am Gabriel. I stand in the presence of God, and I have been sent to speak to you and to bring you this good news. But now, because you did not believe my words, which will be fulfilled in their time, you will become mute, unable to speak, until the day these things occur."

Meanwhile, the people were waiting for Zechariah, and wondered at his delay in the sanctuary. When he did come out, he could not speak to them, and they realized that he had seen a vision in the sanctuary. He kept motioning to them and remained unable to speak. When his time of service was ended, he went to his home. (Luke 1:8–23)

Cradle-Jews

Luke prepares us for the announcement of John's impending birth in a deliberate way. Zechariah is a priest belonging to the order of Abijah (v. 5a). His wife, John's mother-to-be, is a descendent of Aaron (v. 5b). Both of them are "righteous before God" and they live "blamelessly according to all the commandments and regulations of the Lord" (v. 6). The timing of the appearance is carefully described as well. When Zechariah receives the news, he is, according to custom, offering incense in the sanctuary of the Lord (vv. 8–9) and "the whole assembly of the people [are] praying outside" (v. 10). John's parents could not be more firmly rooted in the tradition, nor could they be better examples of observant cradle-Jews.

Cradle-Jews, like cradle-Episcopalians, were Jews from birth.

Then, when John is born, Zechariah is filled with the Holy Spirit and offers at God's prompting a prophecy that places John's birth at the center of God's saving work and Israel's history:

Blessed be the Lord God of Israel,
for he has looked favourably on his people and redeemed them.
He has raised up a mighty saviour for us
in the house of his servant David,
as he spoke through the mouth of his holy prophets from of old,
that we would be saved from our enemies and from the hand of
all who hate us. Thus he has shown the mercy promised to
our ancestors,
and has remembered his holy covenant,
the oath that he swore to our ancestor Abraham,
to grant us that we, being rescued from the hands of our enemies,
might serve him without fear, in holiness and righteousness
before him all our days.
And you, child, will be called the prophet of the Most High;
for you will go before the Lord to prepare his ways,

to give knowledge of salvation to his people
by the forgiveness of their sins.
By the tender mercy of our God,
the dawn from on high will break upon us,
to give light to those who sit in darkness and in the shadow
    of death,
to guide our feet into the way of peace." (Luke 1:68–79)

In a similar fashion Luke is also careful to emphasize the Jewish credentials of Mary and Joseph. The angel Gabriel is dispatched to deliver the news of Jesus' birth (v. 26). Joseph belongs to "the house of David" (v. 27). Mary is greeted as "favored one" (v. 28) and God will give her son "the throne of David" (v. 32).

> *In a similar fashion Luke is also careful to emphasize the Jewish credentials of Mary and Joseph.*

In the sixth month the angel Gabriel was sent by God to a town in Galilee called Nazareth, to a virgin engaged to a man whose name was Joseph, of the house of David. The virgin's name was Mary. And he came to her and said, "Greetings, favoured one! The Lord is with you." But she was much perplexed by his words and pondered what sort of greeting this might be. The angel said to her, "Do not be afraid, Mary, for you have found favour with God. And now, you will conceive in your womb and bear a son, and you will name him Jesus. He will be great, and will be called the Son of the Most High, and the Lord God will give to him the throne of his ancestor David. He will reign over the house of Jacob for ever, and of his kingdom there will be no end." (Luke 1:26–33)

Then, as Zechariah does with John the Baptist, Mary frames in prophetic terms the place of Jesus in the history of Israel and the saving acts of God:

"My soul magnifies the Lord,
and my spirit rejoices in God my Saviour,
for he has looked with favour on the lowliness
    of his servant.
Surely, from now on all generations will call
    me blessed;
for the Mighty One has done great things
    for me,

> *Then, as Zechariah does with John the Baptist, Mary frames in prophetic terms the place of Jesus in the history of Israel and the saving acts of God.*

and holy is his name.
His mercy is for those who fear him
from generation to generation.
He has shown strength with his arm;
he has scattered the proud in the thoughts of their hearts.
He has brought down the powerful from their thrones,
and lifted up the lowly;
he has filled the hungry with good things,
and sent the rich away empty.
He has helped his servant Israel,
in remembrance of his mercy,
according to the promise he made to our ancestors,
to Abraham and to his descendants for ever." (Luke 1:46b–55)

Jesus was a good Jewish boy from a devout, observant Jewish family.

A Widening Circle of Witnesses

As anyone knows who has ever been through a Christmas pageant, the witnesses to the place of Jesus in Jewish history and tradition increases in number as time goes on. In succession we are introduced to the shepherds (2:8ff.); "an angel of the Lord" (2:9–14); Simeon, who is not just a witness to the Gentiles who will listen, but to Israel which will be glorified (2:25–35); and Anna, who speaks to those who "await the redemption of Jerusalem" (2:36–38). It is a diverse group, but they all possess one kind of Jewish credential or another and they all speak to the quintessentially Jewish credentials of Jesus.

As a youth, even Jesus himself confirms what has been said about him. He is in Jerusalem for Passover every year (2:41). He is frequently in the Temple, discussing the law with the rabbis (v. 46); and when his anxious parents express their frustration in losing him, he retorts that the Temple is where he needed to be (v. 49).

The widening circle of witnesses to the birth of Jesus all possess one kind of Jewish credential or another and they all speak to the quintessentially Jewish credentials of Jesus himself.

Eventually, John the Baptist's testimony is added to the chorus, framing his own mission and that of Jesus in terms of Israel's history (3:1ff.). The Holy Spirit descends upon Jesus at his baptism (v. 22a), and God adds his own word of witness (v. 22b).

The entire chorus of those proclaiming Jesus' true identity are Jews or servants of the Most High God of Israel.

Then—noting that Jesus is now thirty and beginning his work—Luke adds a genealogy that further cements his Jewish credentials, his place in the history of Israel, and his messianic claim (3:23–38). This genealogy, unlike the one in Matthew (who was a Jewish Christian) moves backward instead of forward, and it includes Adam, which masterfully underlines the connection with things Jewish and Gentile as well as the universal claims of the gospel.

Ending Where It All Began

The same themes surface again at the end of Luke's gospel on the road to Emmaus (24:13ff.) and the story ends where it all began:

Now on that same day two of them were going to a village called Emmaus, about seven miles from Jerusalem, and talking with each other about all these things that had happened. While they were talking and discussing, Jesus himself came near and went with them, but their eyes were kept from recognizing him. And he said to them, "What are you discussing with each other while you walk along?" They stood still, looking sad. Then one of them, whose name was Cleopas, answered him, "Are you the only stranger in Jerusalem who does not know the things that have taken place there in these days?" He asked them, "What things?" They replied, "The things about Jesus of Nazareth, who was a prophet mighty in deed and word before God and all the people, and how our chief priests and leaders handed him over to be condemned to death and crucified him. But we had hoped that he was the one to redeem Israel. Yes, and besides all this, it is now the third day since these things took place. Moreover, some women of our group astounded us. They were at the tomb early this morning, and when they did not find his body there, they came back and told us that they had indeed seen a vision of angels who said that he was alive. Some of those who were with us went to the tomb and found it just as the women had said; but they did not see him." Then he said to them, "Oh, how foolish you are, and how slow of heart to believe all that the prophets have declared! Was it not necessary that the Messiah should suffer these things and then enter into his glory?" Then beginning with Moses and all the

The same themes surface again at the end of Luke's gospel on the road to Emmaus and the story ends where it all began.

prophets, he interpreted to them the things about himself in all the scriptures. (Luke 24:13–27)

His bewildered disciples don't yet recognize Jesus as they confess their despair at the events surrounding the crucifixion (vv. 19bff.). So he chastises them for their failure to believe what they have learned from the prophets (v. 25) and to understand that the suffering he has experienced was essential to his role as Messiah. Then Jesus reviews his place in salvation history as it is described in Scripture (v. 27): "Then beginning with Moses and all the prophets, he interpreted to them the things about himself in all the scriptures."

The connection is made again later in the same vignette. The disciples recognize Jesus in the breaking of the bread, and this time, teaching them at length, he focuses on his crucifixion and resurrection. But the reference to Jewish tradition and its relationship to the larger, Gentile church is there as well. Luke writes:

> Then he said to them, "These are my words that I spoke to you while I was still with you—that everything written about me in the law of Moses, the prophets, and the psalms must be fulfilled." Then he opened their minds to understand the scriptures, and he said to them, "Thus it is written, that the Messiah is to suffer and to rise from the dead on the third day, and that repentance and forgiveness of sins is to be proclaimed in his name to all nations, beginning from Jerusalem. You are witnesses of these things. And see, I am sending upon you what my Father promised; so stay here in the city until you have been clothed with power from on high." (Luke 24:44–49)

Naturally, the comments made by Jesus in both passages move the story along. But if you read it imagining that you are hearing them for the first time and that you are listening to the story hungry for some indication that the faith you are embracing is rooted in the tradition, then it also has the effect of reasserting and reviewing truths that *you* are meant to hear as well.

The Journey to Jerusalem

There is, of course, a good deal that transpires in between the beginning and the end in Luke's gospel, and much of that material is organized around Jesus' journey to Jerusalem. This journey doesn't simply surface over time. Luke makes it clear why Jesus has "turned his face to Jerusalem" for this last journey:

> When the days drew near for him to be taken up, he set his face to go to Jerusalem. And he sent messengers ahead of him. On their way they entered a village of the Samaritans to make ready for him; but they did not receive him, because his face was set towards Jerusalem. When his disciples James and John saw it, they said, "Lord, do you want us to command fire to come down from heaven and consume them?" But he turned and rebuked them. Then they went on to another village. (Luke 9:51–56)

There is, of course, a good deal that transpires in between the beginning and the end in Luke's gospel, and much of that material is organized around Jesus' journey to Jerusalem.

Then the obligations of discipleship are summarized in a pointed fashion that is equally definite about what Jesus is asking and why:

> As they were going along the road, someone said to him, "I will follow you wherever you go." And Jesus said to him, "Foxes have holes, and birds of the air have nests; but the Son of Man has nowhere to lay his head." To another he said, "Follow me." But he said, "Lord, first let me go and bury my father." But Jesus said to him, "Let the dead bury their own dead; but as for you, go and proclaim the kingdom of God." Another said, "I will follow you, Lord; but let me first say farewell to those at my home." Jesus said to him, "No one who puts a hand to the plough and looks back is fit for the kingdom of God." (Luke 9:57–62)

Significantly, the announcement of the Jerusalem journey also lies between two critical events: the transfiguration (Luke 9:28–36) and the sending of the seventy (Luke 10:1–16). Luke does not use the Jerusalem-journey motif in a loose or casual fashion. To the contrary, the announcement of the reason for the journey, placed as it is between these two events, serves as a pivotal point in the story he tells.

Up to this point in the gospel Luke has taken us through the inaugural prophecies that set the stage for the ministry of Jesus. He has described his inaugural sermon and he has sketched the constituencies that Jesus has met along the way: Gentiles, Jewish leaders, the crowds, and the prospective disciples.

Now, in *setting* his face to go to Jerusalem, Jesus draws an allusion to the prophetic task of the Son of Man found in the prophecy of Ezekiel. What will follow in sermon, parable, and pronouncement is a ministry that draws some, scandalizes others, and forges a new community. The transfiguration sets the stage for this enterprise by demonstrating that Jesus is a prophet in the tradition of Moses and the sending of the seventy signals its beginnings and its scope.

What will follow in sermon, parable, and pronouncement is a ministry that draws some, scandalizes others, and forges a new community. The transfiguration sets the stage for this enterprise by demonstrating that Jesus is a prophet in the tradition of Moses and the sending of the seventy signals its beginnings and its scope.

Back to the Future

That is why the speech given by Jesus at the end of the gospel not only serves as a fitting end to the whole, but also reveals what the journey to Jerusalem was finally meant to accomplish:

> Then he said to them, "These are my words that I spoke to you while I was still with you—that everything written about me in the law of Moses, the prophets, and the psalms must be fulfilled." Then he opened their minds to understand the scriptures, and he said to them, "Thus it is written, that the Messiah is to suffer and to rise from the dead on the third day, and that repentance and forgiveness of sins is to be proclaimed in his name to all nations, beginning from Jerusalem. You are witnesses of these things. And see, I am sending upon you what my Father promised; so stay here in the city until you have been clothed with power from on high."
>
> Then he led them out as far as Bethany, and, lifting up his hands, he blessed them. While he was blessing them, he withdrew from them and was carried up into heaven. And they worshipped him, and returned to Jerusalem with great joy; and they were continually in the temple blessing God. (Luke 24:44–53)

That is also why on the road to Emmaus, when Jesus recounts the saving work of God, the only historical figure that receives specific mention is Moses. Jesus, revealed as the new Moses at the transfiguration, set his face to go to Jerusalem, enlisted seventy elders to begin gathering a new community, and now, in the wake of his death and resurrection, his followers wait for the Holy Spirit to accomplish that mission.

That is why the speech given by Jesus at the end of the gospel not only serves as a fitting end to the whole, but also reveals what the journey to Jerusalem was finally meant to accomplish.

It is that community to which Luke's church belongs. It is new, to be sure, but it is also grounded in the tradition that is the saving work of the God of Israel. So at the end they are where they were at the beginning—back in the Temple and waiting for the next chapter of the story of which they are a part to begin.

Tradition and Newness

Respect for tradition does not keep Jesus from hearing God or from hearing the demands of the kingdom in new ways. Nor does Luke shrink from challenging those approaches to tradition that rob people of a capacity to respond to God.

In the stories he tells in the run up to the transfiguration and the mission of the seventy, as well as those he relates in the course of the journey to Jerusalem, Luke describes Jesus taking an approach that cuts across the Jewish traditions while at the same time acknowledging their place in Israel's history with God. The themes are not overly systematized and the absence of some kind of tight outline no doubt reflects the complexity of Jesus' ministry and Luke's own desire to treat the witness from which he is working in an orderly fashion (Luke 1:1, 3). The lack of a systematic explanation of those themes no doubt reflects Luke's desire to simply address the "why, how, and now what?" that his church is struggling with, and to instruct them in the shape of the faith of which they are a part.

> Respect for tradition does not keep Jesus from hearing God or from hearing the demands of the kingdom in new ways.

In that regard, it is clear from the material that Luke includes that neither he nor Jesus believed that a commitment to tradition precluded the ability to attend to new movements of the Holy Spirit. The result, according to Luke, was a ministry and approach to teaching marked by what has been called the life of *a religious original*—someone who may belong to a tradition, but who revolutionizes the way it is understood and lived. In that sense the Jesus of Luke's gospel and Jesus himself model an approach to tradition that honors it and understands its importance, but understands as well that our misappropriation of it can keep us from God and from God's kingdom.

> It is clear from the material that Luke includes that neither he nor Jesus believed that a commitment to tradition precluded the ability to attend to new movements of the Holy Spirit.

At the conclusion of the mission of the seventy, Jesus explicitly notes that this sense of God's presence is possible. He describes it as characteristic of the coming of the kingdom of God; and in the form of a blessing that promises a bold vision of the future that lies ahead, he vows that his disciples will share in this radical attention to the things of God. The passage is all the more important appearing as it does at the end of their carefully described mission:

> At that same hour Jesus rejoiced in the Holy Spirit and said, "I thank you, Father, Lord of heaven and earth, because you have hidden these things from the wise and the intelligent and have revealed them to infants; yes, Father, for such was your gracious will. All things have been handed over to me by my Father; and no one knows who the Son is except the Father, or who the Father is except the Son and anyone to whom the Son chooses to reveal him." Then turning to the disciples, Jesus said to them privately, "Blessed are the eyes that see what you see! For I tell you that many prophets and kings desired to see what you see, but did not see it, and to hear what you hear, but did not hear it." (Luke 10:21–24)

The particularities of this spiritual vision—eyes that see and ears that hear the truth—are worked out at length on either side of this turning point in the ministry of Jesus and take a variety of forms to which modern and ancient readers need to attend.

Miracles

In some cases the spiritual vision is worked out in the form of miraculous physical cures that also include essential elements of *spiritual* healing. Some of these events establish the immediacy of Jesus' relationship with God and the precedence that it takes over every other consideration. So, for example, in the healing of "the man with an unclean spirit" (4:31–37), the demon protests: "Let us alone! What have you to do with us, Jesus of Nazareth? Have you come to destroy us? I know who you are, the Holy One of God" (v. 34), and the crowd observes,

He describes it as characteristic of the coming of the kingdom of God; and in the form of a blessing that promises a bold vision of the future that lies ahead, he vows that his disciples will share in this radical attention to the things of God.

In some cases the spiritual vision is worked out in the form of miraculous physical cures that also include essential elements of spiritual healing.

"What kind of utterance is this? For with authority and power he commands the unclean spirits, and out they come!" (v. 36).[19]

Other miracles, however, show how Jesus honors tradition but adapts in the moment to express God's mercy. Sometimes that mercy is shown to a person who might otherwise be refused the reconciling love of God because he is not traditionally observant—the leper whom Jesus cleanses (5:12–16) and the centurion's servant whom he heals (7:1–10) are good examples. At other times, as when Jesus heals on the Sabbath (the man with the withered hand in 6:6–11, the man with dropsy in 14:1–6), he seems to defy tradition. But the mercy shown in these healings actually highlights the proper significance and understanding of tradition.

> *Other miracles, however, show how Jesus honors tradition but adapts in the moment to express God's mercy.*

Parables

Parables, especially in Luke's gospel, are an important vehicle for Jesus and they demonstrate the complex interplay between tradition and Jesus' immediate—one might say, transparent—dependence upon God. The parables are attuned to the deep connection between things spiritual and the natural in the daily order of life. Almost all of the parables illustrate one truth or another about the kingdom of God. They are also an important way for Jesus to teach the importance of responding to the presence of God.

> *Parables, especially in Luke's gospel, are an important vehicle for Jesus and they demonstrate the complex interplay between tradition and Jesus' immediate—one might say, transparent—dependence upon God.*

There are a number of parables that show this connection, but perhaps the most important of the parables is the parable of sower:[20]

> When a great crowd gathered and people from town after town came to him, he said in a parable: "A sower went out to sow his seed; and as he sowed, some fell on the path and was trampled on, and the birds of the air ate it up. Some fell on the rock; and as it grew up, it withered for lack of moisture. Some fell among thorns, and the thorns grew with it and choked it. Some fell into good soil, and when it grew, it produced a hundredfold." As he said this, he called out, "Let anyone with ears to hear listen!" (Luke 8:4–8)

In Luke's gospel, parables move into the forefront of Jesus' teaching, and it is in response to questions that his disciples ask that Jesus explains their purpose:

"To you it has been given to know the secrets of the kingdom of God; but to others I speak in parables, so that

'looking they may not perceive,
and listening they may not understand.'"
(Luke 8:9–10)

Here Jesus uses the explanation of his parables to underline the difference between those who are enthralled to tradition and those who honor it but seek the kingdom. Parables invite active looking and listening. But the ability to perceive and to understand depends upon the willingness of the one to whom the parables are told.[21]

Some interpreters have made a great deal of the way in which parables are used by Jesus to cloak the truth, but this misreads the significance of such language. Luke's description of the exchange speaks more directly to the mixed response that Jesus receives among his own followers, the disparity of responses from Jew and Gentile, and the prophetic expectation that when the one sent by God comes, not all will hear and understand the message (Isa 6:9). That is why, according to Jesus, the emphasis from the parable falls on the kind of reception that the preaching of the kingdom receives:

"Now the parable is this: The seed is the word of God. The ones on the path are those who have heard; then the devil comes and takes away the word from their hearts, so that they may not believe and be saved. The ones on the rock are those who, when they hear the word, receive it with joy. But these have no root; they believe only for a while and in a time of testing fall away. As for what fell among the thorns, these are the ones who hear; but as they go on their way, they are choked by the cares and riches and pleasures of life, and their fruit does not mature. But as for that in the good soil, these are the ones who, when they hear the word, hold it fast in an honest and good heart, and bear fruit with patient endurance." (Luke 8:11–15)

Proclamation and Prophetic Acts

Of course, Jesus does not always speak in parables. In Luke's gospel he is often very direct, and much of the tension in his ministry between the necessity of responding to the coming of the kingdom and the place of tradition is worked out in proclamation or prophetic acts:

> At daybreak he departed and went into a deserted place. And the crowds were looking for him; and when they reached him, they wanted to prevent him from leaving them. But he said to them, "I must proclaim the good news of the kingdom of God to the other cities also; for I was sent for this purpose." So he continued proclaiming the message in the synagogues of Judea. (Luke 4:42–44)

Of course, Jesus does not always speak in parables. In Luke's gospel he is often very direct, and much of the tension in his ministry between the necessity of responding to the coming of the kingdom and the place of tradition is worked out in proclamation or prophetic acts.

Here, again, it is important to see the way in which that priority is developed in conversation with the Jewish tradition:

- Jesus speaks in the synagogues (see above).
- Jesus uses the language forms of the tradition (e.g., beatitudes and woes, Luke 6:20bff.; 10:13ff.).
- Jesus challenges the nation by modeling his own call on the twelve tribes of Israel (the sending of the twelve, Luke 9:1ff.).
- Though he lives in considerable tension with the practice there, Jesus—like prophets before him—continues to be in Jerusalem and the Temple (Luke 19:28ff.).

Anti-Semitic, Anti-Jewish, or None of the Above?

Ironically, it is Luke's complex approach to tradition that has opened him to the charge in some quarters that he is anti-Semitic and, if not anti-Semitic, anti-Jewish.[22] This, however, is our problem, not Luke's. It is certainly legitimate to highlight the potential for bigotry and hatred that lies in errant interpretations of the New Testament. But the key phrase is "errant interpretation" and that is something that no text that endures over centuries can guard against. Both the interpretations that lead to bigotry and the ones that project that bigotry onto the text hear what they hear in Luke because they read his gospel at a distance, outside the original circle of storyteller and listener. That distance almost guarantees misunderstanding.

Ironically, it is Luke's complex approach to tradition that has opened him to the charge in some quarters that he is anti-Semitic and, if not anti-Semitic, anti-Jewish. This, however, is our problem, not Luke's.

It is difficult for us to hear what Luke and his readers heard. For them to grapple with the law, the prophets, the place of the Temple, and even the parables (which are typical of rural Galileans, but no less Jewish for all that) was to reconcile a Christian faith that for many was still fundamentally Jewish in its consciousness, though with a growing sense of distance from its origins in Judaism.

It is also important to remember that the language used in the New Testament was not conditioned by Western and post-Holocaust sensibilities. Even the language that Luke uses, which faults some Jews and at times the nation as a whole, is insider language—Jewish language directed at a Jewish audience. You see this sort of language in extrabiblical literature of the day, as well as in the Old Testament— the prophets in particular. Abraham Heschel, who was himself Jewish and remains one of the giants of scholarship in the Hebrew prophets, observed:

> The prophet is intent on intensifying responsibility, is impatient of excuse, contemptuous of pretense and self-pity. His tone, rarely sweet or caressing, is frequently consoling and disburdening; his words are often slashing, even horrid—designed to shock rather than edify. The mouth of the prophet is a "a sharp sword." He is "a polished arrow" taken out of the quiver of God (Isa. 49:2).
>
> > Tremble, you women who are at ease,
> > Shudder, you complacent ones;
> > Strip, and make yourselves bare,
> > Gird sackcloth upon your loins.
> > (Isaiah 32:11)
>
> Reading the words of the prophets is a strain on the emotions, wrenching one's conscience from the state of suspended animation.[23]

Luke is not a prophet, but he writes of things prophetic, about people who are prophets, and about a savior who speaks in prophetic terms. The tradition out of which he writes is steeped in Judaism, speaking to and about a church whose consciousness is thoroughly Jewish. What we find in Luke, then, is not a criticism from without— born of the kind of blind and hateful animosity that fueled the Holocaust—but a striving to understand and follow from within.

Luke as Historian

Of course, a part of what drove him to that struggle was history. In fact, there are numerous scholars of Scripture who have grappled with the question of whether or not Luke is the New Testament's one and only historian. Those who believe he is point to Luke's interest in an orderly account, his attention to distinguishing between eyewitness reports and other kinds of sources, and the lengthy "set speeches" he uses in both his gospel and the book of Acts.

Of course, a part of what drove him to struggle with tradition was history.

Those who disagree note that Luke has an outlook on history that is strongly shaped by Jewish concepts, so that his gospel is more akin to the salvation histories of the Old Testament. His story is grounded in real events, they note, but he is more interested in the theological significance of what happened than in the events themselves.

Both sides are also forced to admit that ancient histories are substantially different from modern histories, regardless of which camp is right in their judgment about Luke's commitments to writing history. The ability to photograph and record events, as well as preserve and uncover material from the past has changed the way we write histories.

We are also committed to writing objective accounts of history. That commitment may be fragile and our ability to be objective is often debatable. We have also seriously blurred the lines between fact and fiction. Historical novels are presumably factual, but they are also fictional, and thanks to the sophistication of computer graphics, we can make things seem to have happened that never did. But our concerns with history and fact do make for a very different way of writing history and a very different set of distinctions between the literature we describe as history and the literature we describe as fiction. By contrast, ancient historians wrote to make a point or offer a moral exemplar. So the lines between history and other kinds of literature were very different from the ones we observe.

I am inclined to believe that Luke was not a historian, but he had an ancient historian's sensibilities. Be that as it may, this much is clear: in unfolding his story, Luke does not pander to his audience or sidestep the plot complications. His is a story of belonging, but it is not easy belonging. He does not ignore the complexity of the past or the ambiguities of the history of Israel.

Luke was not a historian, but he had an ancient historian's sensibilities. Be that as it may, this much is clear: in unfolding his story, Luke does not pander to his audience or sidestep the plot complications. His is a story of belonging, but it is not easy belonging.

Struggling to Understand the Place of Tradition

This commitment to deal with the hard bits of the story forces Luke to struggle with tradition, and his struggle with it can help contemporary readers like us. For us, tradition often has either the power to enthrall or repel. We view it is as either sacred and untouchable, or oppressive and something to be escaped. In the polarized world in which we live, there is often little or no room between the two extremes and the rhetoric around tradition tends to gravitate to one pole or the other.

While I was in the middle of writing this chapter, I bought a bottle of Moroccan mint tea that includes quotations inside the bottle cap. An illustration of our cultural prejudices about tradition was right there on display: "Traditions are group efforts to keep the unexpected from happening."[24] No small number of people would probably add, "Yes, and the bastards are always using it to keep us down!"

Luke, by contrast, struggles with tradition, even though he belongs to a church that might have had good reason to abandon the past. Why Luke chooses to take this much more difficult route, we will never know for certain. Some scholars believe that his comfort with things Jewish is because he was himself a God-fearer and already had close ties to the synagogue. So the connection with Judaism was, for Luke, not something that he could easily discard.

I am inclined to agree. I *suspect*—I can't *know*—that Luke himself was a God-fearer and a *Theophilus*, a lover of God. As such, he wrote (as many of us do) as much to address his own struggles as those of churches to which he wrote. He had heard the law of Moses and the prophets read in the synagogue. He was strongly drawn to the God of Israel, and when he embraced the gospel—as an expression of that

This commitment to deal with the hard bits of the story forces Luke to struggle with tradition, and his struggle with it can help contemporary readers like us.

faith, not as a faith entirely apart—he was drawn into a struggle with the tradition he had already learned.

If he really was one of Paul's companions, furthermore, the association with Paul would also explain Luke's commitment to tradition. After all, no one struggled more with the relationship between Judaism and gospel of Jesus Christ than Paul. Luke, no doubt, would have witnessed Paul's struggle and discovered a model for the way forward.

Whatever the case may be, Luke demonstrates how important the vocabulary of tradition can be—for talking about what is happening in a community, for building bridges to the past and future, and for weighing the legitimacy of the way forward that we choose. One of Luke's gifts to a modern reader is his clarity about the fact that tradition does not necessarily foreclose on the future or on creative responses to God; there have been huge changes in the history of Christianity, but none of them rivals the changes that were taking shape in the early church's understanding of its Jewish origins. Tradition does, however, ground those choices in an obligation to attend to the story told thus far as we look toward the future.

Luke demonstrates how important the vocabulary of tradition can be—for talking about what is happening in a community, for building bridges to the past and future, and for weighing the legitimacy of the way forward that we choose.

A Tradition of One as Opposed to Many

For decades now sociologists have been tracking the deepening influence of individualism and privatization on religion and spiritual practice in the United States. The individual's right of choice has shaped modern spiritual lives that are increasingly idiosyncratic and have prompted large numbers of people to withdraw from any obligation to worshipping communities and traditions they see as unnecessary or oppressive. Instead, they develop their own unique mix of spiritual and religious convictions. Their beliefs might lack the complexity of the Nicene Creed, but that does not make the point any less valid—they have developed a "tradition," a list of core things that they believe and practice in their own personal religion. Traditions are not developed by religious tyrants plotting to put an end to spiritual freedom, but arise out of the spiritual lives of people like you and me because we need them.

Whether we are living out a tradition of our own making, or like millions of still others who remain in traditional faith communities, the fact remains: we need them and in their absence we invent them.

Whether we are living out a tradition of our own making, or like millions of still others who remain in traditional faith communities, the fact remains: we need them and in their absence we invent them. I have a friend who, whenever she urged her children to handle a particular challenge with love, courage, or honesty, would observe, "That's the way Holbrooks do things." Even as adults her children continue to quote their mother—to their own children. But traditions have as much or as little power as they have the ability to provide us with a vocabulary that will allow us to talk to one another about God, build bridges to the past and future, and weigh the legitimacy of our chosen way forward.

What is striking about the spiritual strength and maturity of a religious original like Jesus is that he exercises the kind of freedom that most people never achieve, while remaining deeply involved with his tradition. Likewise, the wisdom of Luke's church was that no matter how difficult their relationship with the past, it needed to be understood in the context of God's saving work.

CHAPTER FOUR

Authority

Not long ago I was involved in a project designed to explore the origins of the church's formative traditions. The people who participated represented a wide variety of churches. What that study helped many of us to see with new insight was the broad range of ways in which the church's traditions take shape. The list included Scripture, creeds, councils, liturgies, sacraments, bishops, saints, teachers, and images.[25] The work we did was intended to explore the wide array of resources that shape our convictions as Christians. We also sought to acknowledge that no matter how long that list of traditions might be, there are still other dimensions of our common life that shape our understanding of the Christian faith. For that reason, the book we produced even talked about the church's "heritage."

But when the question of tradition is in play, the issue of authority is never far behind. It is never just a matter of *what* do we believe? It is also a matter of "What *must* we believe? What parts of the tradition are required? What parts can be

> When the question of tradition is in play, the issue of authority is never far behind. It is never just a matter of what *do we believe?* It is also a matter of "What must *we believe? What parts of the tradition are required? What parts can be rejected?"*

rejected?" As we worked together, we had long conversations about what should and should not be on the list and what does and does not dictate what we believe. That's not surprising. Everything on the list of traditions could be construed as an authority, or as something used by an authority to dictate how the members of a church should conduct themselves or live their lives.

But conversations about authority typically resonate with people in a different way than do conversations about tradition. Talk about tradition and you *might* have a polite conversation about the past. Talk about authority and conversations become more volatile and a new set of issues emerges. You will find yourself being told, "You must choose—between law and grace, order and spirit, discipline and freedom, orthodoxy and mercy." Authority is always an issue in discussions of faith, even when no one uses the word itself.

Luke and Questions of Authority

It is not surprising, then, to find that the question of authority surfaces in Luke's gospel. The issues of authority, of course, were already there, long before Luke began to write.

It is not surprising, then, to find that the question of authority surfaces in Luke's gospel. The issues of authority, of course, were already there, long before Luke began to write:

- By what authority did Jesus teach what he taught?
- By what authority did he act in the way that he did?
- By what authority did he claim what he claimed—for himself and on behalf of God?

There was no way for Luke to write about the ministry and teaching of Jesus without addressing those issues, even if all he did was quote what Jesus had said. But to grapple with the relationship of a dominantly Gentile church to the Jewish tradition out of which it arose was to inevitably raise an added set of questions about authority:

To grapple with the relationship of a dominantly Gentile church to the Jewish tradition out of which it arose was to inevitably raise an added set of questions about authority.

- By what authority did Paul, Luke, and others admit Gentiles to what was still largely a Jewish sect?

- By what authority were Gentiles allowed to exercise a different kind of freedom with regard to the Jewish law?
- If Gentiles had responded in larger numbers to a gospel largely ignored by the vast majority of Palestinian Jews, what authority did the gospel itself possess?

Luke takes two volumes—his gospel and the book of Acts—to answer those questions, but all the basic answers are covered in one way or another in his gospel.

Luke and Appeals to Authority

Luke did not answer these questions in the way they are outlined here. That's hard to do in a story. What he does do, however, is refer to three kinds of authority that he felt were basic to the story he told:

> Luke did not answer these questions in the way they are outlined here. That's hard to do in a story. What he does do, however, is refer to three kinds of authority that he felt were basic to the story he told.

- The authority of the God of Israel
- The authority of prophecy
- The authority of the Messiah

Differences in Debates about Authority: Ancient and Modern

If you have ever raised children, you know that it is very important to figure out what they really want to know when they ask a question—especially if it is a question about sex. Otherwise, you will answer a question that is not being asked.

The same dilemma occurs when reading Scripture, though the challenge is a bit different. Ancient communities often asked and answered questions we don't typically ask. When we read the Bible, what we often see is the answer to those questions. The challenge, then, is to avoid assuming that *their* answer is the answer to *our* question rather than their own.

So it is with the issue of authority. Ancient religious communities and individual writers in particular often asked a different set of questions about authority than the ones we ask today. We run the risk of misunderstanding the significance of their answers if we do not

Ancient religious communities and individual writers in particular often asked a different set of questions about authority than the ones we ask today. We run the risk of misunderstanding the significance of their answers if we don't understand how different their questions were.

understand how different their questions were. In reading Luke there are three important differences:

1. More often than not, when we talk about religious authority, we are really asking the question, "Can you prove that there is a God?" To the extent that Luke talked about the claims his faith might make on the lives of others, his question was "Why is your god the 'best' god?" We are the product of an intellectual heritage that has nurtured doubt and skepticism as the royal road to knowledge. We are also exposed to large numbers of people who believe in other gods, or don't believe in a god at all. So proof that God exists is often more important to us. In the ancient world, however, people often took the existence of God for granted. So debates between religious communities assumed the form of a debate over the claims of one god versus another.

2. When we talk about the claims that religious authority makes on our lives, we usually ask, "Why should God's will change the way *I* live?" In Luke's world, the question was "Why should God's will change the way *we* live? Our questions are individual in character; his were corporate and communal. In the modern Western world, we talk a great deal about what we as individuals should do and why. Rights figure prominently in our conversation; obligations much less so. It is harder to get us to talk about the theological justifications for what we believe. This tends to be the case in part because the individual is the defining unit in a liberal democracy. Frankly, we never get around to caring about the communal aspects of what we believe, or we pick and choose what we submit to communal scrutiny—because neither is particularly important to us. In all fairness, that is largely because it is much harder to imagine that kind of communal accountability to authority. In the ancient world, even to be in conversation with "the world" was a matter of being in conversation with a very small world. Today, to have a conversation with our world does still not include everyone, but it includes far more people and perspec-

tives than ever before. By contrast, the essential questions for Luke were communal in nature, with individual questions secondary in nature. This was accentuated by the diverging lives of Jewish and Gentile communities. Both communities still worshiped the same God and, in a very real sense, even today the conversation between Jews and Christians feels like a conversation about the same God. But Luke's question did revolve around the question of what does God want from God's people; and Luke was obliged to answer that question.

3. As a result, for Luke the other question is the one frequently asked of Jesus, "By what authority do you do these things?" Judging from the book of Acts and Paul's epistles, the questions about the church's authority and the claims made for Jesus by the church were very much alive among early Christians. Luke would not have necessarily isolated this issue of authority as one among others, but it was always there, nonetheless. It was a question that Jewish Christians asked Luke and his Gentile church; and Luke answered this question seamlessly and intuitively as a part of the story he tells.

As we listen, it is worth remembering the differences. We may not always be sympathetic with Luke's argument. He would not be sympathetic with all of ours. But reading his gospel obligates us to understand him.

> As we listen, it is worth remembering the differences.

Authority of the God of Israel

I have a friend who was fond of saying, "Her Majesty and I abhor name-dropping." For religious people, however, particularly those who belong to the same community, there is no God like our God. Name-dropping is a common phenomenon.

If the legitimacy of the Gentile mission was at stake, there could be no appeal to authority that exceeded the appeal to God's will. To make the case that the God of Israel was the author of both the ministry of Jesus and the reconciliation of Gentiles was to make the strongest in-group appeal Luke could make.

> If the legitimacy of the Gentile mission was at stake, there could be no appeal to authority that exceeded the appeal to God's will.

It's not surprising, then, to find that Luke immediately appeals to the authority of the God of Israel. In the birth of John the Baptist, beginning with Luke 1:5, we are made aware of the fact that Zechariah and Elizabeth have the very best sorts of roots in the story of Israel (v. 5) and are righteous before God and obedient to his commandments (v. 6). Zechariah is serving in the Temple of the Lord (v. 9) and an angel of the Lord confronts him *at* the altar (v. 11). The mission that will make Zechariah's son, John, "great in the sight of the Lord" (v. 15) and his task—which we now already know is authorized by the God of Israel —will also turn the people of Israel to their God (vv. 16 and 17).

Pity poor Zechariah. He is not given much time to adjust. He points out that all of this is a bit difficult to believe, given his age and Elizabeth's, but in short order, the angel responds:

> "I am Gabriel. I stand in the presence of God, and I have been sent to speak to you and to bring you this good news. But now, because you did not believe my words, which will be fulfilled in their time, you will become mute, unable to speak, until the day these things occur." (Luke 1:19–20)

This is not just a garden-variety angel—it is one that "stands in the presence of God." (One is tempted to ask, "Is there another kind?") But the point is clear: the author of all that is about to transpire is the God of Israel.

This point will be made repeatedly throughout Luke's gospel, and there is no need to endlessly unpack the examples that could be cited. But this first passage illustrates how important this appeal is for Luke; how much it is a part of his own religious consciousness. It is not just a calculated literary device; it is the way Luke thinks. The authority of the God of Israel weaves its way through every paragraph of Luke's gospel.

But the point is clear: the author of all that is about to transpire is the God of Israel.

Beyond this, the other place that Luke makes an implicit but pointed appeal to the authority of the God of Israel is in chapter 20. In this critical point in the gospel, Jesus has arrived at last in Jerusalem and he begins to teach. Notice how many ways the story appeals to the authority of the God of Israel:

One day, as he was teaching the people in the temple and telling the good news, the chief priests and the scribes came with the elders and said to him, "Tell us, by what authority are you doing these things? Who is it who gave you this authority?" He answered them, "I will also ask you a question, and you tell me: Did the baptism of John come from heaven, or was it of human origin?" They discussed it with one another, saying, "If we say, 'From heaven,' he will say, 'Why did you not believe him?' But if we say, 'Of human origin,' all the people will stone us; for they are convinced that John was a prophet." So they answered that they did not know where it came from. Then Jesus said to them, "Neither will I tell you by what authority I am doing these things."

He began to tell the people this parable: "A man planted a vineyard, and leased it to tenants, and went to another country for a long time. When the season came, he sent a slave to the tenants in order that they might give him his share of the produce of the vineyard; but the tenants beat him and sent him away empty-handed. Next he sent another slave; that one also they beat and insulted and sent away empty-handed. And he sent yet a third; this one also they wounded and threw out. Then the owner of the vineyard said, 'What shall I do? I will send my beloved son; perhaps they will respect him.' But when the tenants saw him, they discussed it among themselves and said, 'This is the heir; let us kill him so that the inheritance may be ours.' So they threw him out of the vineyard and killed him. What then will the owner of the vineyard do to them? He will come and destroy those tenants and give the vineyard to others." When they heard this, they said, "Heaven forbid!" But he looked at them and said, "What then does this text mean:

'The stone that the builders rejected
has become the cornerstone'?

Everyone who falls on that stone will be broken to pieces; and it will crush anyone on whom it falls." When the scribes and chief priests realized that he had told this parable against them, they wanted to lay hands on him at that very hour, but they feared the people. (Luke 20:1–19)

As a matter of reverence, ancient Jews often avoided using the name of God and relied on "circumlocutions"—talking around the subject of God in order to mention the subject of God. So when in the back and forth of the verbal sparring with Jesus, they realize that they cannot admit that John's ministry is "from heaven," they are trying to avoid saying, "The God of Israel authorized John's ministry."

New Testament scholar Luke Timothy Johnson does an excellent job of summarizing all that Luke accomplishes by placing this story here: from here to Acts, chapter 7, all of the action will take place in Jerusalem. The central issue will be whether or not the people are willing to receive God's prophet and (I would add) God's son. Luke has also cast the confrontation in a form that makes perfect sense, both to those who understand Jewish debates between rabbis and those who understand Gentile debates between philosophers, by using the kind of arguments and the style of debate that both would have recognized. So not only does the story ring true to its original setting, it also would speak to the Gentile audience to which his gospel is addressed. To top it all off, Luke has also begun to explain why Jesus was finally crucified.[26]

Of course what Luke plainly does, both in the exchange with the elders and in the parable of wicked tenants that follows, is address all of the most important questions about the authority of Jesus' ministry and the mission to the Gentiles:

- By what authority did Jesus teach what he taught?
  Answer: The God of Israel.
- By what authority did he act in the way that he did?
  Answer: The God of Israel.
- By what authority did he claim what he claimed—for himself and on behalf of God?
  Answer: The God of Israel.
- By what authority did Paul, Luke, and others admit Gentiles to what was still largely a Jewish sect?
  Answer: The God of Israel.
- By what authority were they allowed to exercise a different kind of freedom with regard to the law?
  Answer: The God of Israel.
- If Gentiles had responded in larger numbers to a gospel largely ignored by the vast majority of Palestinian Jews, what authority did the gospel itself possess?
  Answer: The God of Israel.

Luke's story is actually a far more interesting rendering of the same answer. But as a matter of authority, it was the most important answer he could give and one on which all the other appeals to authority relied.

The presence of the Spirit in the ministry of Jesus confirms the divine authority at work in the events Luke describes.

This is why the work of the Holy Spirit figures so prominently in Luke and particularly in the first four chapters. The presence of the Spirit in the ministry of Jesus confirms the divine authority at work in the events Luke describes. Before his birth the gospel notes that John will be filled with the Holy Spirit (1:15). The Spirit moves on Mary in the conception of Jesus (1:35). The Spirit prompts Elizabeth (1:41), Zechariah (1:67), and Simeon (2:25–27) to speak prophetically about Jesus. The Spirit rests upon Jesus at his baptism (3:22), drives him into the desert (4:1), and rests upon him at the inauguration of his ministry (4:18). He rejoices in the Holy Spirit at the manifestations of the kingdom's coming when the disciples inaugurate the mission to the Gentiles (10:21), and the Spirit is promised to those who believe (11:13). The possibility of sinning against the Spirit underlines the authority of the work that God is doing (12:10). We are told that the Spirit is charged with teaching the fledgling church (12:12) and (less directly) we are told that the disciples were instructed to wait until they were clothed with the power of the Spirit (24:49).

Authority of Prophecy

Prophecy, if it is genuine, is given at the direction of God. As such, the authority that prophets exercise is unmediated. So it is not surprising to find that Luke also makes early and frequent references to the authority of prophecy, connecting it to both the ministry of Jesus and the mission to the Gentiles. The references he makes to prophecy take one of three forms:

Luke also makes early and frequent references to the authority of prophecy, connecting it to both the ministry of Jesus and the mission to the Gentiles.

1. In some places he refers to the fulfillment of Old Testament prophesies.
2. In some he describes John the Baptist and Jesus as prophets.
3. In still other places he refers to prophecies made by Jesus that are fulfilled elsewhere in Luke-Acts.

Luke uses the first form of appeal at the very beginning of the gospel. He indicates in the first chapter and the first verse that he plans to write about "the events that have been fulfilled." From that point on, much of what happens is a fulfillment of prophetic expectation. Sometimes Luke uses a specific a prophetic text (3:4ff), sometimes he alludes to imagery found in the prophets (1:16–17), and in still other cases he describes events as that which "must" have happened (24:44).

It is easy for modern readers to misunderstand Luke's reasoning here. For the casual reader it is easy to assume that his logic runs this way:

- Something was predicted in the distant past that no one but God could have anticipated.
- It has happened.
- So it must be God's work.

But prophetic "proofs" of this kind are a peculiarly modern and Western preoccupation. They are also typical of cultures in which the existence of the divine is in question. Usually what people are thinking when they read Luke this way has more to do with proofs for God's existence than anything else. So the logic runs:

- Something was predicted in the distant past that no one but God could have anticipated.
- It has happened.
- So it must be God's work.
- *And* because this kind of thing happens, God exists.

By contrast, in the ancient world there was no question that God was at work in the world, so there was little interest in proofs of this kind. Few people would have thought they were necessary. Rather than ask, "Does God exist?" they asked, "What is God doing?" That is why Scripture recycles prophesies from the past with no sense that their lack of fulfillment presents a problem. Prophecies were not crystal-ball phenomena, and prediction-fulfillment patterns were not what concerned Luke or his readers.

In the ancient world there was no question that God was at work in the world, so there was little interest in proofs of this kind. Few people would have thought they were necessary. Rather than ask, "Does God exist?" they asked, "What is God doing?"

The original Greek meant more than the fulfillment of certain predictions. Instead, it refers to something that "fully realizes" an expectation or hope. In all likelihood, then, what Luke had in mind was something more like this:

- We have longed and looked for this for a long time.
- Now it is here in all its fullness.
- This is God's work.

It is in this sense that the ministry of Jesus and the mission to the Gentiles fulfill prophetic expectations.

As I said at the outset, however, the ministry of John and Jesus is not just the subject matter of prophecy. John and Jesus also wear the mantle of prophet.

John's ministry is modeled on the prophecy of Isaiah:

"The voice of one crying out in the wilderness:
'Prepare the way of the Lord,
make his paths straight.
Every valley shall be filled,
and every mountain and hill shall be made low,
and the crooked shall be made straight,
and the rough ways made smooth;
and all flesh shall see the salvation of God.'"
(Luke 3:4b–6)

> *The ministry of John and Jesus is not just the subject matter of prophecy. John and Jesus also wear the mantle of prophet.*

"The word of the Lord" comes to him (3:2). He speaks as a prophet and acts like a prophet (3:7ff.). Luke is explicit about John's prophetic role and in a later passage Jesus himself confirms John's prophetic credentials:

When John's messengers had gone, Jesus began to speak to the crowds about John: "What did you go out into the wilderness to look at? A reed shaken by the wind? What then did you go out to see? Someone dressed in soft robes? Look, those who put on fine clothing and live in luxury are in royal palaces. What then did you go out to see? A prophet? Yes, I tell you, and more than a prophet. This is the one about whom it is written,

'See, I am sending my messenger ahead of you,
who will prepare your way before you.'

I tell you, among those born of women no one is greater than John; yet the least in the kingdom of God is greater than he." (Luke 7:24–28)

The ministry of Jesus is also modeled on a prophet. This time the model is Moses. Like Moses, he is filled with the Holy Spirit and driven into the wilderness (4:1). He gathers twelve disciples to represent the twelve tribes of Israel (9:1–6). He organizes seventy disciples to proclaim the coming of the kingdom among the nations, recalling Moses' decision to appoint the elders to assist in governing the children of Israel (10:1–16) He teaches the law (e.g., 6:1–5, 6–11). When Jesus recounts the saving acts of God and the history of Israel, he begins with Moses (24:27, 44). When he is transfigured, Moses is present as a sign that the prophetic mantle has passed from him to Jesus (9:28–36).

Jesus does much more than simply emulate Moses, however. He is explicit about the ways in which his own ministry is not an imitation but a realization of prophetic expectations in all their fullness.

Jesus does much more than simply emulate Moses, however. He is explicit about the ways in which his own ministry is not an imitation but a realization of prophetic expectations in all their fullness. Angelic visitors remind his grieving followers:

"Why do you look for the living among the dead? He is not here, but has risen. Remember how he told you, while he was still in Galilee, that the Son of Man must be handed over to sinners, and be crucified, and on the third day rise again." (Luke 24:5b–7)

It is not easy for modern readers to understand why Luke would be so interested in the prophetic nature of Jesus' ministry. Popular understandings of the prophets gravitate to one of two extremes. Some think of them as fortune-tellers—like magicians, only religious. They foresee divine judgment and unexpected changes in history.

It is not easy for modern readers to understand why Luke would be so interested in the prophetic nature of Jesus' ministry.

Others think of them as social critics or political activists. Prophets are an ancient version of a community organizer or street protester. They lobby for the poor, criticize the rich, and challenge the status quo. If prophets amounted to no more than one of these types, then it would be hard to understand the comparisons made with Jesus, unless—of course—Jesus was him-self either a magician or a politician. And there have been scholars and others who have made that argument.

The problem with that argument and with both these models of prophet is that neither one really captures what ancient prophets were and did. Prophets were "forth-tellers"—messengers of God's truth—not fortune-tellers. They challenged ancient Israel to be faithful to its calling as the people of God. Thus when prophets announced that the wrong course of action would bring judgment, or that a faithful response would be treated in kind by God, they were not predicting the future. They were describing the conse-quences of the nation's behavior in ways that were mostly consistent with God's past dealings with Israel.

While the prophets were often critical of national leadership, moreover, they were not prosecuting a political agenda. They were issuing a theological challenge to a nation that was both body politic and religion, rolled into one. Their overriding con-cern was that Israel be "the people of God"; that obligation became the touchstone of the challenge that they issued. They took their cues not from a political, economic, or social agenda, but from the conviction that the will of God for the people of Israel mattered above all else.

When we remember that Jesus is also challenging the nation of Israel to ask itself what it means to be the peo-ple of God, then it becomes clear that to express this kind of challenge involved being a prophet and to lodge this kind of challenge as Messiah required being the prophet par excellence.

That said, it can still be hard to understand why Luke makes so much of Jesus as prophet if—as is clear elsewhere—he understands him to be Mes-siah. But when we remember that Jesus is also challenging the nation of Israel to ask itself what it means to be the people of God, then it becomes clear that to express this kind of challenge involved being a prophet and to lodge this kind of challenge as Messiah required being the prophet par excellence. You and I may need a savior, and we might want a social critic, but those roles have no necessary connection to one another in the world in which we live. That wasn't the case for Jesus—or for Luke. The two were intertwined. That is why the authority of prophecy mattered.

Authority of the Messiah

It is as Messiah, where the authority of God and the authority of prophecy is brought to bear in the ministry of Jesus.

This is not to say that the role of Jesus as Messiah is of less than primary importance. It is as Messiah, in fact, where the authority of God and the authority of prophecy is brought to bear in the ministry of Jesus. In Jesus all three forms of authority find their focus and fulfillment. Luke describes Jesus as exercising a ministry that is marked by that messianic authority:

■ It is begins with the witness of God at his baptism:

> Now when all the people were baptized, and when Jesus also had been baptized and was praying, the heaven was opened, and the Holy Spirit descended upon him in bodily form like a dove. And a voice came from heaven, "You are my Son, the Beloved; with you I am well pleased." (Luke 3:21–22)

■ It continues as the Spirit guides and shapes his ministry:

> Jesus, full of the Holy Spirit, returned from the Jordan and was led by the Spirit in the wilderness, where for forty days he was tempted by the devil. He ate nothing at all during those days, and when they were over, he was famished. The devil said to him, "If you are the Son of God, command this stone to become a loaf of bread." Jesus answered him, "It is written, 'One does not live by bread alone.'"
>
> Then the devil led him up and showed him in an instant all the kingdoms of the world. And the devil said to him, "To you I will give their glory and all this authority; for it has been given over to me, and I give it to anyone I please. If you, then, will worship me, it will all be yours." Jesus answered him, "It is written,
>
> 'Worship the Lord your God,
> and serve only him.'"
>
> Then the devil took him to Jerusalem, and placed him on the pinnacle of the temple, saying to him, "If you are the Son of God, throw yourself down from here, for it is written,
>
> 'He will command his angels concerning you,
> to protect you,'
> and
> 'On their hands they will bear you up,
> so that you will not dash your foot against a stone.'"

Jesus answered him, "It is said, 'Do not put the Lord your God to the test.'" When the devil had finished every test, he departed from him until an opportune time.

Then Jesus, filled with the power of the Spirit, returned to Galilee, and a report about him spread through all the surrounding country. He began to teach in their synagogues and was praised by everyone. (Luke 4:1–15)

■ The disciples and the crowds are moved to comment upon the self-evident messianic nature of Jesus' ministry:

He went down to Capernaum, a city in Galilee, and was teaching them on the sabbath. They were astounded at his teaching, because he spoke with authority. In the synagogue there was a man who had the spirit of an unclean demon, and he cried out with a loud voice, "Let us alone! What have you to do with us, Jesus of Nazareth? Have you come to destroy us? I know who you are, the Holy One of God." But Jesus rebuked him, saying, "Be silent, and come out of him!" When the demon had thrown him down before them, he came out of him without having done him any harm. They were all amazed and kept saying to one another, "What kind of utterance is this? For with authority and power he commands the unclean spirits, and out they come!" And a report about him began to reach every place in the region. (Luke 4:31–37)

■ And even Jesus' critics are forced to admit that his behavior bears the marks of something that if it were not authorized by God is, by definition, blasphemy:

One day, while he was teaching, Pharisees and teachers of the law were sitting nearby (they had come from every village of Galilee and Judea and from Jerusalem); and the power of the Lord was with him to heal. Just then some men came, carrying a paralysed man on a bed. They were trying to bring him in and lay him before Jesus; but finding no way to bring him in because of the crowd, they went up on the roof and let him down with his bed through the tiles into the middle of the crowd in front of Jesus. When he saw their faith, he said, "Friend, your sins are forgiven you." Then the scribes and the Pharisees began to question, "Who is this who is speaking blasphemies? Who can forgive sins but God alone?" When Jesus perceived their questionings, he answered them, "Why do you raise such questions in your hearts? Which is easier, to say, 'Your sins are forgiven you,' or to say, 'Stand up and walk'? But so that you may know that the Son of Man has authority on earth to forgive sins"—he said to the one who was paralysed—"I say to you, stand up and take your bed and go to your home." Immediately he stood up before them, took what he had been lying on, and went to his home, glorifying God. Amazement seized all of them, and they glorified God and were filled with awe, saying, "We have seen strange things today." (Luke 5:17–26)

■ Jesus' messianic authority is also confirmed by his interpretation of the law (Luke 6:1–11), the freedom with which he forgives sins (Luke 5:17–26), and even his influence over the natural order (Luke 8:25b).

As with Luke's appeal to prophetic authority, the evangelist is not trying to provide proofs of his claims of the kind we might expect. The authority of Jesus for the fledgling church is a given, and the conversation even in the larger Jewish community is not a debate over whether or not there is such a thing as a Messiah. They take that for granted. Instead the issue for them is just what kind of Messiah Israel might expect, and whether or not Jesus was that Messiah.

> As with Luke's appeal to prophetic authority, the evangelist is not trying to provide proofs of his claims of the kind we might expect. Instead the issue is just what kind of Messiah Israel might expect, and whether or not Jesus was that Messiah.

So when Luke touches on the messianic claims of Jesus, the case he makes with the larger Jewish community is the case you would make for those who shared that hope: one that is based upon Scripture and reflects the character of Jesus' ministry and teaching.

Within the church and among Gentiles in particular, the question of authority rested ultimately with the witness of the Messiah himself. The fact that Jesus assembled the community of which they were a part, drew the first of them into it, organized the first mission to them, and then set the stage for the chapter of the story that was theirs, made all the difference to people who longed to belong.

> The fact that Jesus assembled the community of which they were a part, drew the first of them into it, organized the first mission to them, and then set the stage for the chapter of the story that was theirs, made all the difference to people who longed to belong.

Authority Then and Now

This is not, of course, to say that there were no tensions arising from Luke's understanding of where and how God was leading the church. The debate over the place of spiritual authority forces us to balance the gifts of the discipline and structure, questions of identity, and the call of the Holy Spirit. The difficulty lies in naming where the balance lies at any one moment in the life of the church (or in our private lives), between law and grace, order and spirit, discipline and freedom, orthodoxy and mercy.

This is not, of course, to say that there were no tensions arising from Luke's understanding of where and how God was leading the church.

Jesus had been accused by the religious establishment of his day of being a blasphemer, of betraying the law, order, discipline, and orthodoxy. Paul joined this chorus in accusing the early disciples of the same failure. Then, in short order, the first generation of converts to the gospel accused people like Paul of being the one who betrayed that balance by baptizing Gentiles into the church without giving due attention to the law. Paul, in turn, found himself cautioning the "strong" in Corinth of playing the freedom card too heavily—and that is just what we know about that early history from a handful of documents. In retrospect, the image of white-water rafting works well to describe the complex debate in which the church of Luke's day discovered itself. It careened in and out of the rough water of the debate over the tensions between authority and spiritual freedom in the space of just a few generations.

In retrospect, the image of white-water rafting works well to describe the complex debate in which the church of Luke's day discovered itself. It careened in and out of the rough water of the debate over the tensions between authority and spiritual freedom in the space of just a few generations.

Those who know church history well know that we continue to navigate in and out of rough water. We can take sides, styling ourselves as the defenders of orthodoxy or spiritual freedom. We can take sides by judging that the church (at its best) is always on one side or the other of such debates. Or we can take sides by judging that the church is always at its worst and on one side or the other of those debates. I have known people who have held all three positions—at once. The problem is that such easy solutions overlook the complex demands that living faithfully makes upon us. To commit ourselves to community is to commit ourselves to some measure of authority; and to live faithfully always means listening to the ever-transcendent demands of God. We need both spiritual roots and spiritual wings.

To commit ourselves to community is to commit ourselves to some measure of authority; and to live faithfully always means listening to the ever-transcendent demands of God. We need both spiritual roots and spiritual wings.

Authority may seem, by definition, opposed to the freedom of spiritual flight, but that depends upon your understanding of authority. For anyone who considers authority no more than the exercise of power or control, then that might be the case. If authority is nothing more than the ability to exercise power, then there are usually only two possibilities in terms of the way that we relate to it. We either wield it, or we are subject to it.

But if authority means the ability to author creativity, if it has something to do with the boundaries that make for healthy, not self-destructive exploration, then the answer might be different. A jazz musician can be marvelously creative, but the greatest of jazz musicians respect the authority of music theory and the proper use of their instruments. Part of what distinguishes musical genius from slavish performances is often the degree of freedom that an instrumentalist exercises within boundaries. Press the formula one direction and you get a performance that is little better than the average first-year student can produce. Press the formula too far in the other direction and you may play music that no one appreciates or that no longer resembles music.

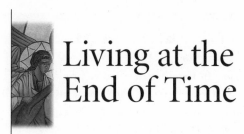

CHAPTER FIVE

Living at the End of Time

Did you ever wonder what your view of life's end has to do with the way you live your life now? Few of us do unless circumstances force us to. A serious illness, a tragic loss, or even a major birthday can get us to think about issues of that kind. But by and large we tend to buy our homes, do our work, and make hundreds of other choices without much thought about how our lives will end—much less how life itself will end.

The result is that the random thoughts we do have about the end of life tend to be a grab bag of impressions. They come from a variety of sources, much of it casual conversation. They rarely develop much beyond the categories of heaven and hell, reward and punishment. As a result, they have very little to do with the rest of what we believe about how we live our lives. The end of life tends to feel like a series of bad jokes or not-so-funny stories about how, having lived life on other terms, we each finally get a thumbs-up or thumbs-down on the lives we have lived.

How Life Ends and How Life Is Lived

It might surprise you to learn, then, that for well over a century scholars have been debating how life choices (or ethics) and the end of all things (eschatology) fit together in the teaching of Jesus. The reason, at least in part, is because Jesus was explicit about both of them in ways that we rarely are.

For well over a century scholars have been debating how life choices (or ethics) and the end of all things (eschatology) fit together in the teaching of Jesus.

Though he had predecessors, the debate began in the last century with physician, biblical scholar, and organist Albert Schweitzer and his groundbreaking book called *The Quest of the Historical Jesus.* Schweitzer noted that Jesus' teaching consisted broadly of two parts. One had to do with how life would end, which was organized around the central concept of the kingdom of God (eschatology), while the second was about how life should be lived (ethics).[27]

What puzzled Schweitzer and what he tried to resolve was the way in which eschatology and ethics fit together. Assuming that Jesus expected the end to come soon, he was hard-pressed to explain why Jesus would also care about how people behaved in the here and now. He finally concluded that Jesus did in fact expect the end of life to come soon—or to put it in language more appropriate to the teaching of Jesus, he expected the kingdom of God to come soon. Schweitzer also argued that Jesus taught people how to behave as a means of preparing for the kingdom, espousing a radical ethic that could only be expected of people who did not believe they had much time to wait for the coming of God. Jesus demanded impossible things from his followers because he knew that the end was coming almost immediately, and everyone could live radically for the short time that was left. Schweitzer called this an "interim ethic," or rules for living just before the end of the world.

Schweitzer's analysis got the debate rolling and it has been rolling ever since. Scholars have offered alternative definitions of what Jesus thought about the end. Some have tried to redefine what they thought the timetable was that Jesus was using. Some have argued that the end Jesus had in mind

What puzzled Schweitzer and what he tried to resolve was the way in which eschatology and ethics fit together.

was metaphorical, not literal. Still others have argued that the *church* was the one interested in the end, and not Jesus at all.

According to Schweitzer Jesus demanded impossible things from his followers because he knew that the end was coming almost immediately.

Sorting through that debate is not really important here. Sorting through how Luke understood the relationship between the end and ethics in the teaching of Jesus *is*—and it might not be a bad guide to how they actually fit together for Jesus, and how they might fit together for us. So over the next two chapters I would like to do four things:

- Look at the way Luke understands time and the coming of the kingdom.
- Define what Jesus and Luke understood the kingdom of God to be.
- Examine the convictions about the coming of the kingdom that shaped Luke's ethic.
- Consider what the conversation might mean for us.

The Kingdom, Time, and Luke

Some years ago a colleague of mine had a sign on his office door that read, "Time is God's way of keeping everything from happening all at once." In a good-natured way it hinted at just how complicated things can get when we talk about God and time. Does God experience time or is God outside time? If God experiences time, is that experience the same as ours? If God is outside time, does God know how it all worked out? If God knows how the story ends, then why bother with the tedium and disappointment of getting us to respond?

One of the problems with Schweitzer's approach is that the answer he offers is too simple. Nowhere is this problem clearer than it is in Luke's gospel.

The century-long debate that Schweitzer started touches on the complex subject of time and God and what God knows, if only on the much more narrow question of when the kingdom is coming. One of the problems with Schweitzer's approach is that the answer he offers is too simple. Nowhere is this problem clearer than it is in Luke's gospel. If one reads Luke carefully, it becomes apparent that:

79

- The kingdom does not belong just to *the immediate future.*
- It belongs to the *present*
- and the *indefinite future.*

Or put another way, the kingdom of God is:

- Here now
- A cause for action in the immediate future
- And the hoped-for work of God.

The Kingdom Is Here Now

From the very beginning of Luke's gospel it is clear: the kingdom is now. Jesus declares the coming of the kingdom:

> *From the very beginning of Luke's gospel it is clear: the kingdom is now.*

At daybreak he departed and went into a deserted place. And the crowds were looking for him; and when they reached him, they wanted to prevent him from leaving them. But he said to them, "I must proclaim the good news of the kingdom of God to the other cities also; for I was sent for this purpose." So he continued proclaiming the message in the synagogues of Judea. (Luke 4:42–44)

There is no specific reference to the coming of the kingdom as present tense here. That is true. But the programmatic announcement that this is his ministry and the purpose for which he was sent is in clear juxtaposition with descriptions of teaching, exorcisms, and healing. Jesus proclaims the kingdom, but he also brings the kingdom. It is already present with him; and its power is already at work in the world.

The seventy returned with joy, saying, "Lord, in your name even the demons submit to us!" He said to them, "I watched Satan fall from heaven like a flash of lightning. See, I have given you authority to tread on snakes and scorpions, and over all the power of the enemy; and nothing will hurt you. Nevertheless, do not rejoice at this, that the spirits submit to you, but rejoice that your names are written in heaven." (Luke 10:17–20)

But the kingdom is more than just present with Jesus. As Messiah, Jesus also embodies the presence of the kingdom as its messenger. So a response to Jesus is not simply necessary because the kingdom is here; a response to Jesus is *defining*. He is not merely the agent of the kingdom's coming, but the embodiment of its coming. When John sends his disciples to ask if Jesus is the one for whom they have waited, Jesus cites his healings and exorcisms—all events anticipated in the messianic age, according to Isaiah (see 29:18–19 and 61:2). But he also stresses the intimate connection between a response to him as Messiah and a willingness to acknowledge that these events signal the arrival of the kingdom:

> *But the kingdom is more than just present with Jesus. As Messiah, Jesus also embodies the presence of the kingdom as its messenger.*

> The disciples of John reported all these things to him. So John summoned two of his disciples and sent them to the Lord to ask, "Are you the one who is to come, or are we to wait for another?" When the men had come to him, they said, "John the Baptist has sent us to you to ask, 'Are you the one who is to come, or are we to wait for another?'" Jesus had just then cured many people of diseases, plagues, and evil spirits, and had given sight to many who were blind. And he answered them, "Go and tell John what you have seen and heard: the blind receive their sight, the lame walk, the lepers are cleansed, the deaf hear, the dead are raised, the poor have good news brought to them. And blessed is anyone who takes no offence at me." (Luke 7:18–23)

The same conversation is said to have prompted Jesus to observe:

> "I tell you, among those born of women no one is greater than John; yet the least in the kingdom of God is greater than he." (And all the people who heard this, including the tax-collectors, acknowledged the justice of God, because they had been baptized with John's baptism. But by refusing to be baptized by him, the Pharisees and the lawyers rejected God's purpose for themselves.) (Luke 7:28–30)

In other words, the coming of Jesus signals the arrival of the kingdom, and his ministry signals a watershed in the history of God's saving work. By contrast, John belongs to the era just before. For that reason, the decision to accept his offer of baptism signals a willingness to prepare for the arrival of both the Messiah and the kingdom of God.

The sayings, parables, and images that Jesus uses also communicate this message. Here, too, many of the same themes are worked out:

- The imperative of responding immediately to the kingdom:

He also said to the crowds, "When you see a cloud rising in the west, you immediately say, 'It is going to rain'; and so it happens. And when you see the south wind blowing, you say, 'There will be scorching heat'; and it happens. You hypocrites! You know how to interpret the appearance of earth and sky, but why do you not know how to interpret the present time?" (Luke 12:54–56)

- The variations in response to the sowing of the word:

"Now the parable is this: The seed is the word of God. The ones on the path are those who have heard; then the devil comes and takes away the word from their hearts, so that they may not believe and be saved. The ones on the rock are those who, when they hear the word, receive it with joy. But these have no root; they believe only for a while and in a time of testing fall away. As for what fell among the thorns, these are the ones who hear; but as they go on their way, they are choked by the cares and riches and pleasures of life, and their fruit does not mature. But as for that in the good soil, these are the ones who, when they hear the word, hold it fast in an honest and good heart, and bear fruit with patient endurance." (Luke 8:11–15)

The sayings, parables, and images that Jesus uses also communicate this message.

- The assertion that if Israel does not respond, Gentiles will:

One of the dinner guests, on hearing this, said to him, "Blessed is anyone who will eat bread in the kingdom of God!" Then Jesus said to him, "Someone gave a great dinner and invited many. At the time for the dinner he sent his slave to say to those who had been invited, 'Come; for everything is ready now.' But they all alike began to make excuses. The first said to him, 'I have bought a piece of land, and I must go out and see it; please accept my apologies.' Another said, 'I have bought five yoke of oxen, and I am going to try them out; please accept my apologies.' Another said, 'I have just been married, and therefore I cannot come.' So the slave returned and reported this to his master. Then the owner of the house became angry and said to his slave, 'Go out at once into the streets and lanes of the town and bring in the poor, the crippled, the blind, and the lame.' And the slave said, 'Sir, what you ordered has been done, and there is still room.' Then the master said to the slave, 'Go out into the roads and lanes, and compel people to come in, so that my house may be filled. For I tell you, none of those who were invited will taste my dinner.'" (Luke 14:15–35)

■ Jesus as one who embodies the presence of the kingdom:

> Once Jesus was asked by the Pharisees when the kingdom of God was coming, and he answered, "The kingdom of God is not coming with things that can be observed; nor will they say, 'Look, here it is!' or 'There it is!' For, in fact, the kingdom of God is among you." (Luke 17:20–21)

In an important sense, then, for Jesus and for Luke the kingdom is here now.

A Cause for Action in the Imminent Future

Of course, when you talk about something that is already here and demands your attention, the next question is, "How long do I have to respond?" Human nature inevitably demands a season, a deadline for decision making.

Of course, when you talk about something that is already here and demands your attention, the next question is, "How long do I have to respond?"

> And he sent messengers ahead of him. On their way they entered a village of the Samaritans to make ready for him; but they did not receive him, because his face was set towards Jerusalem. When his disciples James and John saw it, they said, "Lord, do you want us to command fire to come down from heaven and consume them?" But he turned and rebuked them. Then they went on to another village. As they were going along the road, someone said to him, "I will follow you wherever you go." And Jesus said to him, "Foxes have holes, and birds of the air have nests; but the Son of Man has nowhere to lay his head." To another he said, "Follow me." But he said, "Lord, first let me go and bury my father." But Jesus said to him, "Let the dead bury their own dead; but as for you, go and proclaim the kingdom of God." Another said, "I will follow you, Lord; but let me first say farewell to those at my home." Jesus said to him, "No one who puts a hand to the plough and looks back is fit for the kingdom of God." (Luke 9:52–62)

Some period of time for decision making is often necessary, given the very human demands of communication. Time is needed to declare the message, to make it known, to have it heard.

Some period of time for decision making is often necessary, given the very human demands of communication.

> "Now the parable is this: The seed is the word of God. The ones on the path are those who have heard; then the devil comes and takes away the word from their hearts, so that they may not believe and be saved. The

ones on the rock are those who, when they hear the word, receive it with joy. But these have no root; they believe only for a while and in a time of testing fall away. As for what fell among the thorns, these are the ones who hear; but as they go on their way, they are choked by the cares and riches and pleasures of life, and their fruit does not mature. But as for that in the good soil, these are the ones who, when they hear the word, hold it fast in an honest and good heart, and bear fruit with patient endurance." (Luke 8:11–15)

It takes time to see how lasting the initial response might be. What is more, hearing is not the same as understanding. Decisions of great moment require time and consideration. Jesus is a prophet demanding immediate response. He is also a teacher trying

Jesus is a prophet demanding immediate response. He is also a teacher trying to help people think through their decision.

to help people think through their decision. Some of the time that is needed is part and parcel of the process. The kingdom, as Jesus understands it, is being revealed. It is here in part; it is yet to be here in all its fullness.

Then he said to them, "These are my words that I spoke to you while I was still with you—that everything written about me in the law of Moses, the prophets, and the psalms must be fulfilled." Then he opened their minds to understand the scriptures, and he said to them, "Thus it is written, that the Messiah is to suffer and to rise from the dead on the third day, and that repentance and forgiveness of sins is to be proclaimed in his name to all nations, beginning from Jerusalem. You are witnesses of these things. And see, I am sending upon you what my Father promised; so stay here in the city until you have been clothed with power from on high." (Luke 24:44–49)

It will take time for the gospel of repentance and forgiveness to be known throughout the world. This kingdom spreads with the preaching of the gospel. The proclamation of the kingdom has two stages— first a challenge to the house of Israel and later an announcement to the nations.

Jesus went through one town and village after another, teaching as he made his way to Jerusalem. Someone asked him, "Lord, will only a few be saved?" He said to them, "Strive to enter through the narrow door; for many, I tell you, will try to enter and will not be able. When once the owner of the house has got up and shut the door, and you begin to stand outside and to knock at the door, saying, 'Lord, open to us,' then in reply he will say to you, 'I do not know where you come from.' Then you will begin to say, 'We ate and drank with you, and you taught in our streets.' But he will say, 'I do not know where you come from; go away from me, all you evildoers!' There will be weeping and gnashing of teeth when you see Abraham and Isaac and Jacob and all the prophets in the kingdom of God, and you yourselves thrown out. Then people will come from east and west, from north and south, and will eat in the kingdom of God." (Luke 13:22–29; cf. Acts 28)

The language that Jesus uses can be explained, too, as the fairly natural language of prophetic announcement. For the Hebrew prophets there was no sharp distinction between a present reality and the imminent future. When the cause for taking action is clear, the need to act is imminent. Naturally, the prophets frequently cited the consequences that lay just ahead, if the nation failed to respond.

> *The language that Jesus uses can be explained, too, as the fairly natural language of prophetic announcement.*

There is no particular reason to believe that Jesus did not intend to do the same thing in his prophetic pronouncements. There is even less reason to believe that Luke did not think of it this way. Luke lived and wrote fifty or more years after the ministry of Jesus. He knew what Jesus had said; he knew that there were signs of the kingdom's presence; and he knew that its fulfillment lay in the indefinite and undefined future. That knowledge would have made it impossible for Luke to see the nature of the kingdom in the terms an interim and radical ethic such as Schweitzer imagined.

The Kingdom as the Hoped-for Work of God

This is not to say that Luke does not have another, final, and future reality in mind when he thinks of the kingdom of God. Clearly Luke hopes for a future in which prevailing realities will be reversed and the coming of the kingdom will bring about reconciliation. This hope can be heard in Luke's version of the Sermon on the Mount.

> *This is not to say that Luke does not have another, final, and future reality in mind when he thinks of the kingdom of God.*

Then he looked up at his disciples and said:

"Blessed are you who are poor,
for yours is the kingdom of God.

85

'Blessed are you who are hungry now,
for you will be filled.
'Blessed are you who weep now,
for you will laugh.

"Blessed are you when people hate you, and when they exclude you,
revile you, and defame you on account of the Son of Man. Rejoice on
that day and leap for joy, for surely your reward is great in heaven; for
that is what their ancestors did to the prophets. (Luke 6:20–23)

And the great expectation for the reconciliation of all to God can be
heard in parables like the one about the lost sheep:

Now all the tax-collectors and sinners were coming near to listen to
him. And the Pharisees and the scribes were grumbling and saying,
"This fellow welcomes sinners and eats with them." So he told them
this parable: "Which one of you, having a hundred sheep and losing
one of them, does not leave the ninety-nine in the wilderness and go
after the one that is lost until he finds it? When he has found it, he lays
it on his shoulders and rejoices. And when he comes home, he calls
together his friends and neighbours, saying to them, 'Rejoice with me,
for I have found my sheep that was lost.' Just so, I tell you, there will be
more joy in heaven over one sinner who repents than over ninety-nine
righteous people who need no repentance." (Luke 15:1–7; cf. vv. 8–15)

When we seek to motivate people to change, we necessarily appeal
to ideals that are yet to be realized. We draw on a dreamed-of and, as
yet, unrealized hope. What we offer is a vision of the future. Luke, too,
is clearly aware of the importance of a hoped-for future as a means of
framing both the present and the imminent future. This can make it
difficult to determine where and when Luke is addressing the immediate future, and where and when he is drawing on that as yet unrealized hope. In many, if not most, cases, however, it does not matter. We
have to make decisions that accord with the direction of our hopes;
and to talk about hope inevitably entails talking
about decisions that need to be made soon. To
make decisions for the future requires us to take
our hopes into account. As soon as we do, decisions
come into play that will also change our present;
once the present has been changed, nothing will
ever be the same again—or should be.

We have to make decisions that accord with the direction of our hopes; and to talk about hope inevitably entails talking about decisions that need to be made soon.

Think, for example, of the choices that a prima ballerina makes. (I'm a former ballet-dad with seven years of exposure to that world through my daughter.) Long before a prima ballerina achieves central roles in larger performance venues, she faces a lifetime of choices that take a hoped-for future into account. Endless practice, attention to detail and form, diet and exercise shape her life. Viewed in isolation, the individual sacrifices that she makes could be described as fanatical. But take into account the way in which she understands her life's work and the logic of her effort becomes clear. The hoped-for future shapes her life's choices now.

The same—and more—should be said of the hope that shapes the life of a believer. I take a group of students to St. Gregory's monastery in Shawnee, Oklahoma, each year and the students pray their way through a large part of the Psalter in the space of a week. This year at 6 a.m. vigils they read a passage of Psalm 14 that reflects the complete conviction that our faith can shape our lives if we take it seriously along with the incomprehension of those who do not share that faith. The psalmist writes:

See how they (evil-doers) tremble with fear
Without cause for fear:
For God is with the just.
You may mock the poor man's hope,
But his refuge is the Lord.[28]

The conviction that the kingdom is both here and on its way here is the burden of the language that Jesus uses to describe the decision that faces his hearers.

The conviction that the kingdom is both here and on its way here is the burden of the language that Jesus uses to describe the decision that faces his hearers. It is not a rejection of other loves or the goodness of life's relationships. It is not the urgency of impending judgment overcoming good sense. It is language about the defining nature of a choice to take seriously the coming of the kingdom—put in stark language in order to underline the true nature of the situation in which Israel lives:

As they were going along the road, someone said to him, "I will follow you wherever you go." And Jesus said to him, "Foxes have holes, and birds of the air have nests; but the Son of Man has nowhere to lay his head." To another he said, "Follow me." But he said, "Lord, first let me go and bury my father." But Jesus said to him, "Let the dead bury their own dead; but as for you, go and proclaim the kingdom of God." Another said, "I will follow you, Lord; but let me first say farewell to those at my home." Jesus said to him, "No one who puts a hand to the plough and looks back is fit for the kingdom of God." (Luke 9:57–62)

Luke is hardly a wide-eyed messenger of apocalypse. It is clear at the end of both the gospel and the book of Acts that an apocalyptic end is not Luke's primary concern. He writes instead of the work of the Holy Spirit that has transpired in Jerusalem and beyond:

> *Luke is hardly a wide-eyed messenger of apocalypse. He writes instead of the work of the Holy Spirit that has transpired in Jerusalem and beyond.*

Then he said to them, "These are my words that I spoke to you while I was still with you—that everything written about me in the law of Moses, the prophets, and the psalms must be fulfilled." Then he opened their minds to understand the scriptures, and he said to them, "Thus it is written, that the Messiah is to suffer and to rise from the dead on the third day, and that repentance and forgiveness of sins is to be proclaimed in his name to all nations, beginning from Jerusalem. You are witnesses of these things." (Luke 24:44–48)

The end of the book of Acts anticipates an indeterminate future and a Gentile mission that is nowhere near its end:

After they had fixed a day to meet him, they came to him at his lodgings in great numbers. From morning until evening he explained the matter to them, testifying to the kingdom of God and trying to convince them about Jesus both from the law of Moses and from the prophets. Some were convinced by what he had said, while others refused to believe. So they disagreed with each other; and as they were leaving, Paul made one further statement: "The Holy Spirit was right in saying to your ancestors through the prophet Isaiah,

'Go to this people and say,
You will indeed listen, but never understand,
and you will indeed look, but never perceive.
For this people's heart has grown dull,
and their ears are hard of hearing,
and they have shut their eyes;
so that they might not look with their eyes,
and listen with their ears,

and understand with their heart and turn—
and I would heal them.'

Let it be known to you then that this salvation of God has been sent to the Gentiles; they will listen." He lived there for two whole years at his own expense and welcomed all who came to him, proclaiming the kingdom of God and teaching about the Lord Jesus Christ with all boldness and without hindrance. (Acts 28:23–31)

Clearly, for Luke there is a sense that the story of the church is ongoing, not something coming to an abrupt end. How, then, do we visualize his understanding of time and the kingdom? Scholars use the phrase "realized eschatology": the end is here, but not in its fullness. Another phrase is "already, not yet." Both mean that we live in the space where the future has been forever changed by Christ, but is not yet completely fulfilled.

The end is here, but not in its fullness.

Another and perhaps more memorable way of visualizing when and how the kingdom will come according to Luke is to imagine a sunrise. The kingdom, like a sunrise, is on the move. Light breaks across the landscape. In some places there is already a considerable amount of light present and there is a great deal we can see. In other places shadows remain, objects obscure the sun's progress. But we know that midday is coming and eventually the sun's light will fill the landscape.

Like any other image, it has limitations and it should not be pressed too hard. Luke himself is not specific about how much of the kingdom is present now, or how much of it remains to be fulfilled. It is enough, he might argue, to know that it is already with us and on its way. It is the work Christ began in his earthly ministry and continues in the world through this very day.

Luke and the Kingdom of God

What is the kingdom of God?

In part the answer depends on whether the word "kingdom" (and the Greek behind it, *basileia*) refers to a *place* or to the *activity* of reigning or ruling. At first, that seems like a silly distinction. Every reigning king has a place the king rules over. The

What is the kingdom of God? In part the answer depends on whether the word "kingdom" (and the Greek behind it, basileia) refers to a place or to the activity of reigning or ruling.

king of England, the king of France, and the king of Siam were all monarchs with territories. We know they reigned; we know *where* they reigned.

But it is a bit more difficult than that when we begin talking about the kingdom of God. Nothing Luke tells us about the ministry of Jesus suggests that Jesus occupied a parcel of land and declared, "This is what God will control." He wandered the countryside and preached, he moved from place to place. He did not assert control over anyone who heard him. It is not even clear that he was particularly interested in whether or not God occupied the land of Israel.

We could, of course, think of place in metaphorical terms. If Jesus healed a leper, or preached and a hundred people converted, then we could talk about the leper or the one hundred people as the place where God is in control. But people move around; they may respond to the kingdom of God with one part of their lives, but not with another. That makes it difficult to talk about the kingdom of God as a place, even in metaphorical terms.

If we think of the kingdom as the reign or rule of God, much more falls into place.

If, by contrast, we think of the kingdom as the reign or rule of God, much more falls into place. If (as I have already noted) the kingdom is like the rising sun—fully present here, not there—already, not yet—then it makes more sense to ask "Is God reigning or ruling?" than it does to get stuck on the question of place. It is also the question that makes more sense given the debate in which Jesus found himself embroiled and Luke found himself writing a gospel. In first-century Palestine, kingdom as a place was a problematic concept. First-century Jews could tell you where Israel was. It had familiar borders, the city of Jerusalem and the Temple were intact, and Temple rituals were observed.

But they lived with the memory of exile and endured the domination of the Romans. They had control over their affairs—but only to the extent that the Romans allowed them to control their affairs. They worshiped as they saw fit—but only because the Romans allowed them to worship. They also knew from experience that they could lose their homes and find themselves scattered to the four winds. So the question, "*Where* does God reign?" was difficult to answer in geographical terms. If place was essential to God's reign, then why were these Romans in God's land? That is why, as we have seen, Jesus, the Pharisees, and Zealots were locked in a debate about how to answer the question. If geography had been the heart of the issue, then the question would not have been so difficult to answer.

It was equally difficult for Luke to answer that question in geographical terms. By the time he wrote his gospel, Jews were again scattered. The city of Jerusalem had been sacked, the Temple destroyed. The emerging church of his day was scattered across the Mediterranean. The Gentiles who were being baptized did not belong to the same racial or ethnic family; Christianity was on its way to becoming a worldwide phenomenon. *Where* the kingdom of God could be found was already a difficult question to answer and it was on its way to becoming more difficult to answer. "*Is God reigning or ruling?*" was a far more important question and it had an answer.

The growth of the kingdom of God in the hearts of those who respond depends upon the willingness of those who hear the message and to abandon their attachment to those things that might keep them from responding.

So the kingdom of God is God reigning, ruling—in the hearts of the people of God, in the hearts of individuals. That reign has begun with the ministry of Jesus. A response to his ministry is the measure of one's willingness to enter that kingdom. The growth of the kingdom of God in the hearts of those who respond depends upon the willingness of those who hear the message and to abandon their attachment to those things that might keep them from responding.

> A certain ruler asked him, "Good Teacher, what must I do to inherit eternal life?" Jesus said to him, "Why do you call me good? No one is good but God alone. You know the commandments: 'You shall not commit adultery; You shall not murder; You shall not steal; You shall not bear false witness; Honour your father and mother.'" He replied, "I have kept all these since my youth." When Jesus heard this, he said to him, "There is still one thing lacking. Sell all that you own and distribute the money to the poor, and you will have treasure in heaven; then come, follow me." But when he heard this, he became sad; for he was very rich. (Luke 18:18–23)

To ignore the urgency of the summons to the kingdom runs the risk of judgment that inevitably follows as a consequence of a refusal to heed the spiritual signs that signal the kingdom's arrival. It is not always obvious whether those consequences belong to the immediate future or to the end of all things. Nor is it clear whether the judgment to come will fall on the people of Israel as a whole or on individuals. Consequences for the immediate future as well as for the end time, for the whole people of God and for individuals, often appear together in Luke's gospel as it does in this passage:

> To ignore the urgency of the summons to the kingdom runs the risk of judgment that inevitably follows as a consequence of a refusal to heed the spiritual signs that signal the kingdom's arrival.

> At that very hour some Pharisees came and said to him, "Get away from here, for Herod wants to kill you." He said to them, "Go and tell that fox for me, 'Listen, I am casting out demons and performing cures today and tomorrow, and on the third day I finish my work. Yet today, tomorrow, and the next day I must be on my way, because it is impossible for a prophet to be killed away from Jerusalem.' Jerusalem, Jerusalem, the city that kills the prophets and stones those who are sent to it! How often have I desired to gather your children together as a hen gathers her brood under her wings, and you were not willing! See, your house is left to you. And I tell you, you will not see me until the time comes when you say, 'Blessed is the one who comes in the name of the Lord.'" (Luke 13:31–35)

Whether the judgment is on the nation or on individuals, however, this much is obvious: the decision to respond to the kingdom's coming needs to be made now. The kingdom is unfolding, here and now. The immediate and indefinite future are changed by the transformation of the present. Circumstances are forever changed and it is time to live in response to the reign of God:

> The decision to respond to the kingdom's coming needs to be made now. Circumstances are forever changed and it is time to live in response to the reign of God.

> He also said to the crowds, "When you see a cloud rising in the west, you immediately say, 'It is going to rain'; and so it happens. And when you see the south wind blowing, you say, 'There will be scorching heat'; and it happens. You hypocrites! You know how to interpret the appearance of earth and sky, but why do you not know how to interpret the present time? (Luke 12:54–56)

The defining character of God's reign, of course, rests with the character of God. One of the shortcomings of much popular theology is the tendency to think of the gospel only as a matter of individual redemption, and the kingdom of God as the place where all those who are redeemed end up belonging. Popular theology that tends to think of the kingdom as a *place* misses Luke's point.

The defining character of God's reign rests with the character of God.

Ancient Jewish and early Christian writings are not concerned in the first place with the kingdom of God as the gathering place of the redeemed. The driving force behind the coming of the kingdom is, in the first place, the vindication of God's character and presence: God must be God. The will of God must prevail.

In ancient literature the spiritual well-being of the individual depends upon the vindication of God's claim to be God. If the individual is to prosper spiritually, God must first triumph. That is why there is so much emphasis upon the vindication of God in connection with passages that also celebrate the deliverance of the nation:

If the individual is to prosper spiritually, God must first triumph.

> In the fifteenth year of the reign of Emperor Tiberius, when Pontius Pilate was governor of Judea, and Herod was ruler of Galilee, and his brother Philip ruler of the region of Ituraea and Trachonitis, and Lysanias ruler of Abilene, during the high-priesthood of Annas and Caiaphas, the word of God came to John son of Zechariah in the wilderness. He went into all the region around the Jordan, proclaiming a baptism of repentance for the forgiveness of sins, as it is written in the book of the words of the prophet Isaiah,
>
> > "The voice of one crying out in the wilderness:
> > 'Prepare the way of the Lord,
> > make his paths straight.
> > Every valley shall be filled,
> > and every mountain and hill shall be made low,
> > and the crooked shall be made straight,
> > and the rough ways made smooth;
> > and all flesh shall see the salvation of God.'" (Luke 3:1–6)

If the vindication of God matters, then an all-important question becomes, "What is God like?" Knowing what God is like will tell us something about the kingdom that is both here and coming in all its fullness.

The answer to the question of what God is like is consistent with what was already known about God. For example, Luke and Jesus obviously presuppose that the God we are talking about is the God of Israel, as the reviews of God's saving work reveals more than once (Luke 1:46–56; 1:67–80; 24:25–27, 44–48). It is also clear that this is the same God who established a covenant with Israel, gave it the law, instituted the Sabbath, and can be characterized as holy. So all of these characteristics are undoubtedly reflected in the kingdom:

Luke and Jesus obviously presuppose that the God we are talking about is the God of Israel.

- It is shaped by covenant—an intimate relationship of authority and responsibility between God and God's people.
- It is shaped by the values reflected in the law, or Torah.
- It is a reign in which Sabbath rest is observed and the lordship of the one who brings the kingdom is acknowledged.
- It is a reign where God's people pursue the holiness that reflects the holiness of God.

But for Luke and for Jesus before him, the God whose character shapes the kingdom is also a God in whose kingdom the observance of the law is conditioned by attention to the redemptive purposes of God:

> On another sabbath he entered the synagogue and taught, and there was a man there whose right hand was withered. The scribes and the Pharisees watched him to see whether he would cure on the sabbath, so that they might find an accusation against him. Even though he knew what they were thinking, he said to the man who had the withered hand, "Come and stand here." He got up and stood there. Then Jesus said to them, "I ask you, is it lawful to do good or to do harm on the sabbath, to save life or to destroy it?" After looking around at all of them, he said to him, "Stretch out your hand." He did so, and his hand was restored. But they were filled with fury and discussed with one another what they might do to Jesus. (Luke 6:6–11)

The circumstances of the poor, the hungry, those who grieve, and the reviled are reversed:

> Then he looked up at his disciples and said:

"Blessed are you who are poor,
for yours is the kingdom of God.
"Blessed are you who are hungry now,
for you will be filled.
"Blessed are you who weep now,
for you will laugh.

"Blessed are you when people hate you, and when they exclude you, revile you, and defame you on account of the Son of Man. Rejoice on that day and leap for joy, for surely your reward is great in heaven; for that is what their ancestors did to the prophets." (Luke 6:20–23)

Those who are ritually unclean and unacceptable are admitted:

Now there was a woman who had been suffering from hemorrhages for twelve years; and though she had spent all she had on physicians, no one could cure her. She came up behind him and touched the fringe of his clothes, and immediately her hemorrhage stopped. Then Jesus asked, "Who touched me?" When all denied it, Peter said, "Master, the crowds surround you and press in on you." But Jesus said, "Someone touched me; for I noticed that power had gone out from me." When the woman saw that she could not remain hidden, she came trembling; and falling down before him, she declared in the presence of all the people why she had touched him, and how she had been immediately healed. He said to her, "Daughter, your faith has made you well; go in peace." (Luke 8:43–48)

An ethic of love prevails:

"But I say to you that listen, Love your enemies, do good to those who hate you, bless those who curse you, pray for those who abuse you. If anyone strikes you on the cheek, offer the other also; and from anyone who takes away your coat do not withhold even your shirt. Give to everyone who begs from you; and if anyone takes away your goods, do not ask for them again. Do to others as you would have them do to you." (Luke 6:27–31)

A Conversation with Luke's Gospel

Time is not an absolute with an existence all its own, though clocks, calendars, timers, and stopwatches might give us that impression. We measure it differently from our ancestors who used sundials and, before them, those who simply followed the sun's movements through

Time is not an absolute with an existence all its own, though clocks, calendars, timers, and stopwatches might give us that impression.

the sky. Time will one day be measured with greater precision and in ways that differ from the way in which we measure it now.

Time is also shaped by the hundred and one assumptions we bring to the passing seconds, minutes, hours, and days. Some of those assumptions are culturally conditioned. I worked for a time in Jerusalem and friends often told me that Palestinians live in an "IBM culture"—I for *Inshallah*, "if God wills," B for *Bucra*, "later," and M for *Mallesh*, "it doesn't matter." It is a set of cultural assumptions that creates a completely different approach to the passage of time. Meetings start more slowly, people approximate the starting time, and (by Western standards) everything is either more relaxed or less efficient, depending upon your perspective.

But even within a single culture, judgments about what time it is vary greatly. For example, what it means to be early, late, or on time depends upon the assumptions that we bring to the passage of time. I am sitting in an airport right now. If I had arrived here with less than forty-five minutes to spare, the airline would have considered me late. They might have even given my seat away. They would have pointed to the difficulties in handling my baggage and getting me through security. From my point of view, however, I would have been on time, even early for my flight. The airlines build extra time into their schedules for departure and arrival. So while they are sometimes late, even by their own standards, they are actually "on time" far more often than their passengers think they are.

Jesus and Luke were not convinced that people understood what time it was. They would have argued (and did, in a sense) that time is not just socially constructed, but also spiritually constructed.

Jesus and Luke were not convinced that people understood what time it was. They would have argued (and did, in a sense) that time is not just socially constructed, but also spiritually constructed. The prevailing assumptions that shaped the practice of their faith and the living of their lives was conditioned by a failure to observe that the kingdom had come and the world was forever changed.

Jesus and Luke were also convinced that the kingdom was shaped in decisive ways by the assumptions people made about its ruler.

One could argue, in fact, that the central religious debate for both of them revolved around the identity of God as the key to the identity of the people of God.

Thus, the coming of the kingdom was not an event unrelated to life now. It was not about the future coming of a divine referee to decide who had been naughty or nice. The God who now reigns is a God who has a particular character and reigns in a particular fashion that is as relevant now as it will be in the future. Luke was trying to help Christians see this and understand the seriousness and glory of the response they needed to make.

CHAPTER SIX

Living in the Here and Now

What do all these discussions of time and the future have to do with behavior—or ethics—in the kingdom? Does Jesus demand impossible things from his followers because he knows that the end is coming and there isn't much time left? At first it sounds as if it makes sense: imminent expectation—interim ethic. Just a few days ahead—hold on for dear life, love your neighbors, dissolve your bank account, head for the hills. The problem with this kind of ethic, though, is that this is not the way it works out.

What do all these discussions of time and the future have to do with behavior—or ethics—in the kingdom?

First, Luke is really clear: consequences are coming, but that isn't so much a matter of bracing for the future as about recognizing that the present isn't what we thought. The cloud that is as "small as a man's hand" is already on the horizon. What does it matter whether the storm is three minutes, three hours, or three days away (Luke 12:54–56)? The kingdom of God is among you (Luke 17:20–21). If it is, who cares how much longer it is before the light fills the landscape? Wait here. The Holy Spirit is coming and the story will end midstream, with Paul declaring the gospel

(Acts 28:30–31). How much longer is it going to go on? No one knows. But does that matter? We aren't the first to ask, "How long, oh Lord?"—just look at the psalms. But no one knows how long, and Luke does not seem to believe that the length of time should change our behavior.

Second, the strictures on time, it turns out, do not have predictable results. Some people change the way that they live. Some people affirm the values by which they have always lived. Others conclude that they have lived by standards that should not have shaped so much of their lives, and so they adopt new standards.

That is not only the people of Luke's day—that is also you and me. My brother is one of them. Three years ago he was diagnosed with a malignant brain tumor. It cost him his eyesight and his career as a hand surgeon. Nothing has been the same since. On the Tuesday that they ran the MRI, he went to the chief of surgery to tell him and the chief of surgery could not let him operate. The diagnosis suggests that he has less than five years to live. Time will tell. Percentages tell clinicians how to proceed—be aggressive, don't push too hard, do this, don't do that. But it is not much help to the individual. You are 100 percent of whatever happens to you.

It has forced my brother to reexamine his life. But, not so oddly, the narrow timetable has not forced him into a frantic, stoic existence that emphasizes "gutting it out" because the time is short. It has forced him to ask, instead, "What was I thinking?" "What really mattered here?" "How should I have been looking at life?" "Was it necessary to work so many hours?" "Run so hard?" When time is short, the kinds of questions that can be asked are surprising.

"When Is God Coming?" or "Which God Is Coming?"

Jesus announced that the kingdom was here. The possibilities of judgment and salvation were on their way. Some of them would arrive soon, others later.

But what matters most? The question "when?" or the question "who?" If I told you that Martians were coming soon, it might make an impression. You might run around looking for something to use in self-defense or you might look for a course in Martian. If you think there is such a thing as Martians. But if you don't, then the notion that they are coming would have no affect on you at all. There is no point in changing your life for something you do not believe in.

Students of comparative religious ethics make a similar point. Notions of imminent judgment function as a *sanction*—they reinforce a demand for obedience. So *if* you believe that the God who exacts the judgment exists, then the fact that judgment is coming matters—but mostly by way of added incentive, not by way of defining what is expected.

> If *you believe that the God who exacts the judgment exists, then the fact that judgment is coming matters—but mostly by way of added incentive, not by way of defining what is expected. The more basic belief that guides your behavior is your belief in a particular God.*

The more basic belief that guides your behavior is your belief in a particular God. That belief—its content and convictions about the nature of God—is the *authorization* for the demands made. In other words: if I don't believe that the God to whom you appeal exists, then the argument that that God is going to judge me has no effect at all. If I do believe that the God you describe exists and I am committed to that God, then the coming judgment does matter. But knowing who that God is and what that God values is more important to me than the amount of time I have left to respond. In the logic of religious demands, then, what matters most is not *when* God is coming, but *which* God is coming.

Now, arguably, there are exceptions to this pattern. The Shakers, who built celibate co-ed communities scattered across the United States, believed that the end was near. For that reason they swore off sexual relations and lived in communities that were organized around the separation of the sexes. The history of the group suggests that this was acceptable and even the driving force behind at least some of the community's conduct. It was their beliefs about *when* God was coming that led them to organize their communities in a certain way. But the Shakers are an exceptional group; we cannot generalize from that to say that religious groups always organize themselves that way. As far as Luke's understanding of Jesus is concerned, the way we organize our Christian communities and lives all depends upon the rationale for the demands that Jesus offered and his characterization of the kingdom's coming.

One of the problems with Schweitzer's conclusion that Jesus asked the impossible because the end was coming so soon is the way Jesus characterizes the kingdom in Luke's gospel. Luke plainly believed that the immediate future was not the real issue; the kingdom is already present and the future has no definable end. Those judgments both drive the emphasis on the imminent future and render it less important. If the kingdom is already here and here to stay, then the imminent future does not figure as prominently as it would for a group like the Shakers. In a way the end has already started, and for Luke's church that was the point. They were to live as though they were in the middle of the end.

> *The end has already started, and for Luke's church that was the point. They were to live as though they were in the middle of the end.*

My brother responds in the same way. Having been diagnosed with a life-threatening cancer, he sometimes refers to his life as "time-stamped." He tries to live in the present, knowing that he is living in the end.

Guess Who's Coming to Dinner

The other and more basic problem with Schweitzer's argument is this: when Jesus does appeal for radically transformed behavior in Luke's gospel, what finally matters most is *who*, not *when*: the God *who* asks, those *who* believe, and those *who* act accordingly. Take, for example, the parable of the great banquet:

> Then Jesus said to him, "Someone gave a great dinner and invited many. At the time for the dinner he sent his slave to say to those who had been invited, 'Come; for everything is ready now.' But they all alike began to make excuses. The first said to him, 'I have bought a piece of land, and I must go out and see it; please accept my apologies.' Another said, 'I have bought five yoke of oxen, and I am going to try them out; please accept my apologies.' Another said, 'I have just been married, and therefore I cannot come.' So the slave returned and reported this to his master. Then the owner of the house became angry and said to his slave, 'Go out at once into the streets and lanes of the town and bring in the poor, the crippled, the blind, and the lame.' And the slave said, 'Sir, what you ordered has been done, and there is still room.' Then the master said to the slave, 'Go out into the roads and lanes, and compel people to come in, so that my house may be filled. For I tell you, none of those who were invited will taste my dinner.'" (Luke 14:16–24)

Jesus loved a party. He used table fellowship to signal the coming of the kingdom, and the imagery of eating and drinking in his teaching. He hosted meals and taught when he did. It was so much a centerpiece of his ministry that it earned him a reputation for eating with tax collectors, sinners,

> Jesus loved a party. He used table fellowship to signal the coming of the kingdom, and the imagery of eating and drinking in his teaching.

and drunks—and, worse yet, a reputation for being a glutton and drunk himself.[29] There is probably as much truth as poetry to the observation that on the road to Emmaus, his disciples didn't recognize him until he broke the bread at dinner (Luke 24:30ff.). Luke no doubt emphasizes the episode as a prototype of the eucharistic banquet that became the centerpiece of Christian worship.

In one way, none of this is surprising. In the Middle East, dining together, then and now, carries with it symbolic expressions of family, friendship, and reconciliation. It was and is so important, in fact, that heaven was often described as a banquet. What is significant about a story like the parable of the great banquet, however, is the God who shows up at these events. The host has already set the table. The invitations were issued. The original invitees failed to accept. So time is short and God tasks the servants to beat the bushes for new guests.

> But what surfaces more strongly than the imminence of the banquet (and appears for that reason at the end of the story) is the willingness of God to welcome people who were not on the original guest list.

But what surfaces more strongly than the imminence of the banquet (and appears for that reason at the end of the story) is the willingness of God to welcome people who were not on the original guest list. Here and elsewhere, when Jesus makes demands of those who hear him, he appeals to the identity of the God hosting the party, not the time of the party—the *who*, not the *when* is what matters.

So far as Luke's gospel is concerned, then, the imminence of the kingdom is not what matters, but the God who issues the dinner invitations. That God is:

- father and host (6:36; 14:12–24)
- Jewish and invites his family (6:12ff.; 13:31–35)
- eager to reconcile those who were thought to be beyond reconciliation (14:12–14; 15:1–32)

- forgiving (15:17–24)
- loving (6:36)
- boundlessly generous (9:10–17)
- in no doubt about our need for repentance and amendment of life (13:1–5)
- clear that life in the kingdom involves living like the King and Father (6:36)

Ethics or Discipleship?

Getting a dinner invitation from a God like this is no small matter. It is not enough to show up; and it is not enough to comply in a superficial fashion with the host's expectations. This dinner invitation is life-changing and all-consuming.

> *Getting a dinner invitation from a God like this is no small matter. It's not enough to show up; and it is not enough to comply in a superficial fashion with the host's expectations. This dinner invitation is life-changing and all-consuming.*

In fact, the word "ethics" is really an inadequate label for the demand that this invitation places upon those who hear it. It is not just a code of behavior I have to follow, nor an aspect of life set apart from what I value most. It is about a fundamental reorientation of life that acknowledges the God of banquets and begins to live life as if the banquet has begun.

That is why the word discipleship captures so much more of what the gospel demands. Discipleship is life in the kingdom of God in all its ramifications and glory:

> Now large crowds were travelling with him; and he turned and said to them, "Whoever comes to me and does not hate father and mother, wife and children, brothers and sisters, yes, and even life itself, cannot be my disciple. Whoever does not carry the cross and follow me cannot be my disciple. For which of you, intending to build a tower, does not first sit down and estimate the cost, to see whether he has enough to complete it? Otherwise, when he has laid a foundation and is not able to finish, all who see it will begin to ridicule him, saying, 'This fellow began to build and was not able to finish.' Or what king, going out to wage war against another king, will not sit down first and consider whether he is able with ten thousand to oppose the one who comes against him with twenty thousand? If he cannot, then, while the other is still far away, he sends a delegation and asks for the terms of peace.

So therefore, none of you can become my disciple if you do not give up all your possessions." (Luke 14:25–33)

Torah and the God of Mercy

Because Jesus was a good Jew and Luke lived in a Gentile church that still had strongly Jewish roots, the law figures prominently in conversations about life in the kingdom. The debates that were started in the early church would eventually define two distinctive religious self-understandings—one organized around the risen and resurrected Christ, the other organized around observance of Torah. But those were changes that would stretch out over the next century. For that reason, in Luke's church there were considerable debates both within the fledgling movement and with the rest of Judaism.

> Because Jesus was a good Jew and Luke lived in a Gentile church that still had strongly Jewish roots, the law figures prominently in conversations about life in the kingdom.

Luke relates conversations between Jesus and his fellow Jews that acknowledge the continued importance of the law. There are confrontations over the Sabbath, disputes over ritual purity, and debates over the question of which groups can be classified as ritually clean. Without setting the law aside, Jesus insists on the priority of mercy:

> On one occasion when Jesus was going to the house of a leader of the Pharisees to eat a meal on the sabbath, they were watching him closely. Just then, in front of him, there was a man who had dropsy. And Jesus asked the lawyers and Pharisees, "Is it lawful to cure people on the sabbath, or not?" But they were silent. So Jesus took him and healed him, and sent him away. Then he said to them, "If one of you has a child or an ox that has fallen into a well, will you not immediately pull it out on a sabbath day?" And they could not reply to this. (Luke 14:1–6)

> Without setting the law aside, Jesus insists on the priority of mercy.

Jesus is also insistent upon the significance of love:

> "'If you love those who love you, what credit is that to you? For even sinners love those who love them. If you do good to those who do good to you, what credit is that to you? For even sinners do the same. If you lend to those from whom you hope to receive, what credit is that to you?

Jesus is also insistent upon the significance of love.

Even sinners lend to sinners, to receive as much again. But love your enemies, do good, and lend, expecting nothing in return. Your reward will be great, and you will be children of the Most High; for he is kind to the ungrateful and the wicked." (Luke 6:32–35)

And what is the defining and authoritative nature of the Father's conduct?

> Be merciful, just as your Father is merciful. (Luke 6:36)

Life in the Kingdom as God's Work

The approach to the law that Luke describes would have honored the role of the law, while his emphasis on mercy would have been intelligible and plausible in a dominantly Gentile community still working through the complexities of its relationship with Judaism. But it would be a mistake to think of Luke's approach to the life of discipleship as a matter of individual achievement or solitary response, or to think of Jesus' teaching as a collective expression of individual efforts.

But it would be a mistake to think of Luke's approach to the life of discipleship as a matter of individual achievement or solitary response, or to think of Jesus' teaching as a collective expression of individual efforts.

Life among the reconstituted people of God is the work of God—accomplished through the death, resurrection, and ascension of his Son—and empowered by the Holy Spirit. That is why the journey to Jerusalem is orchestrated so carefully by Luke. In the last of his parables before entering Jerusalem, Jesus frames the events that are about to transpire, highlighting his own role, the resistance of the Jewish leadership, and the reconstitution of the people of God in language that is startling, but typically prophetic:

> As they were listening to this, he went on to tell a parable, because he was near Jerusalem, and because they supposed that the kingdom of God was to appear immediately. So he said, "A nobleman went to a distant country to get royal power for himself and then return. He summoned ten of his slaves, and gave them ten pounds, and said to them, 'Do business with these until I come back.' But the citizens of his country hated him and sent a delegation after him, saying, 'We do not want this man to rule over us.' When he returned, having received royal

power, he ordered these slaves, to whom he had given the money, to be summoned so that he might find out what they had gained by trading. The first came forward and said, 'Lord, your pound has made ten more pounds.' He said to him, 'Well done, good slave! Because you have been trustworthy in a very small thing, take charge of ten cities.' Then the second came, saying, 'Lord, your pound has made five pounds.' He said to him, 'And you, rule over five cities.' Then the other came, saying, 'Lord, here is your pound. I wrapped it up in a piece of cloth, for I was afraid of you, because you are a harsh man; you take what you did not deposit, and reap what you did not sow.' He said to him, 'I will judge you by your own words, you wicked slave! You knew, did you, that I was a harsh man, taking what I did not deposit and reaping what I did not sow? Why then did you not put my money into the bank? Then when I returned, I could have collected it with interest.' He said to the bystanders, 'Take the pound from him and give it to the one who has ten pounds.' (And they said to him, 'Lord, he has ten pounds!') 'I tell you, to all those who have, more will be given; but from those who have nothing, even what they have will be taken away. But as for these ene-mies of mine who did not want me to be king over them—bring them here and slaughter them in my presence.'" (Luke 19:11–27)[30]

The power of this parable to frame the future as Luke describes it in his gospel cannot be underestimated. It presupposes the events that are about to follow, announces the salvation and judgment that will ensue, and highlights the role of Jesus. The same themes are echoed in the passion narrative that follows, stressing the way in which the death, resurrection, and ascension accomplish those ends:

- the triumphal entry (19:28–40, esp. vv. 37–40);
- the observations of Jesus as he weeps over Jerusalem (19:41–44);
- the debate with the chief priests, scribes, and elders over his authority (20:1–8);
- the parable of the vineyard and the tenants (20:9–18);
- the warning Jesus gives about the leadership of the scribes (20:45–47);
- the warnings about the destruction of the Temple and Jerusalem (21:5–6, 20–24);
- the coming of the Son of Man foretold (21:25–28);

- the lesson of the fig tree (21:29–33);
- the exhortation to watch (21:34–36);
- the institution of the Lord's Supper, as modeled on the Feast of Passover (22:14–20);
- the debate between Jesus and the Council (22:66–71);
- the interview of Jesus by Pilate (23:1–5);
- the words of Jesus to the daughters of Jerusalem (23:28–31);
- the words of forgiveness spoken by Jesus from the cross (23:32–34);
- the ironic words of the soldiers and the sign nailed to the cross (23:35–38);
- the words of forgiveness spoken by Jesus to the criminal on the cross (23:43);
- the words of Jesus to the Father (23:46);
- the words of Jesus to the women at his grave (24:5–7);
- and the words of Jesus to the disciples on the road to Emmaus (24:25–27, 30–35, 44–48)

When the story is told in this fashion, Jesus is not the victim of opposing forces but the instrument of God. Jesus enters the events of Passion Week with the same purposefulness that marked the journey to Jerusalem. Reflecting on the parable of the king and his kingdom that announced it all, one commentator observes:

> Who is the nobleman . . . ? It is obviously Jesus himself. . . . Who are the fellow citizens who do not wish to have this one as their ruler . . . ? They are the leaders of the people who will decry the proclamation of Jesus as king, accuse him of royal pretensions in his trial, mock him as king on the cross, reject his mission as prophet, persecute his apostles, and find themselves at last because of all of this, "cut off from the people." Who are the servants whose faithful use of possessions is rewarded by *exousia* . . . ["authority"] within the realm of this king? The Twelve, whom we shall see in the narrative of Acts exercising just such authority over the restored people of God.[31]

A Different Kind of Belonging

Is all of this conversation about making choices and reconstituting the people of God a needless complication of the theme of belonging that, as we have already seen, was so important to Luke and his church? As it turns out, no. Luke does not believe in belonging without responsibility. For Luke, belonging to the kingdom required acknowledging the importance of tradition, accountability to spiritual authorities, and living a life shaped by a way of being that reflected the God who calls us all. Love could not be had without the truth, belonging could not be had without discipleship, reconciliation could not be had without repentance. Luke sought to define the gift and the obligation that are part and parcel of belonging to God. That is why the reference Luke makes to Jesus teaching his disciples to pray is not incidental to his story, but central to the kind of belonging that matters:

> For Luke, belonging to the kingdom required acknowledging the importance of tradition, accountability to spiritual authorities, and living a life shaped by a way of being that reflected the God who calls us all.

> He was praying in a certain place, and after he had finished, one of his disciples said to him, "Lord, teach us to pray, as John taught his disciples." He said to them, "When you pray, say:
>
> Father, hallowed be your name.
> Your kingdom come.
> Give us each day our daily bread.
> And forgive us our sins,
> for we ourselves forgive everyone indebted to us.
> And do not bring us to the time of trial." (Luke 11:1–4)

Radically at odds with our own preoccupation with prayers of personal petition, the prayer that Jesus teaches his disciples to say is devoted to the things of God and to the coming of God's kingdom. It is the Father's name that should be hallowed. It is the coming of the kingdom for which they are to pray. Belonging is not sought for its own sake.

Some years ago a member of the monastic community that I visit annually was elected president of the university that the monastery founded. Father Lawrence is a young man and was even younger when he was chosen for this great responsibility and the local newspaper was understandably interested in his story. In the course of the interview, the reporter asked a typical question and received an unusual answer. "What is your ambition?" the reporter asked. Pointing to the cemetery outside the monastery abbey, Father Lawrence responded, "To end up out there."

He was not being morbid. Father Lawrence understood that monastic life is an outpost of the kingdom of God and it nurtures the same belonging to God that is part and parcel of life in the kingdom: belonging that redeems our lives, bears us up, gives us direction, and offers enduring hope.

But it is also the kind of belonging that makes a claim upon our lives and requires us to act in the here and now. We are not simply loved and accepted, we are trusted. To be trusted brings with it shared responsibility for building the kingdom of God. As Saint Ignatius of Loyola would teach centuries later, we are loved individually by God, but we are also the beloved companions of God. Companions are not simply comforted, they share in the work of the one who loves them. To belong is to act in the here and now, to extend the reign of God, and to trust in the larger work of God that lies beyond the cemetery where faithful monks—and all of God's children—wait in hope.

ACKNOWLEDGMENTS

No book is ever written without endless debts known and unknown, remembered and forgotten—all inadequately acknowledged. Gratitude for those influences on this volume must include the two men who introduced me to biblical scholarship: Robert W. Lyon and George Bradford Caird, men who lived and taught their passion. For their support of the Conversations series and assistance in preparing this volume: Nancy Fitzgerald, Davis Perkins, Cynthia Shattuck, and Frank Tedeschi. For her tireless attention to editing the first drafts of this manuscript, sage advice, conversation, and encouragement: my wife, Natalie, who is, in her own right, a priest and scholar. Her efforts greatly improved this volume. The remaining defects are, as they say, inevitably mine.

STUDY QUESTIONS

This study of Luke by biblical scholar and spiritual director Frederick Schmidt begins, "Luke had a story to tell and he told his story to change people's lives." From there he invites us into the gospel by focusing on five key themes that are essential to Christians today—the motifs of belonging, tradition, authority, ethics, and the future.

Introduction

Before you begin, pray together for the guidance of the Holy Spirit in this work and study you are about to undertake, using the collect for St. Luke the physician at the beginning of this book. Ask for the grace to proceed with an open and flexible mind so that the encounter with this gospel might truly change you.

Take several hours to read the whole of Luke's gospel in one sitting. Pay attention to what might be familiar in this gospel, such as the stories of the Prodigal Son and the Good Samaritan, and what seems alien or difficult. Note down particular passages that evince strong positive or negative reactions. What do you like best about this gospel? Which parts make you uncomfortable?

Chapter One: Telling the Old, Old Story

Luke's gospel brings with it a spiritual challenge and questions that can be fruitfully pursued in connection with this "old, old story":

- What is the story of your spiritual journey?
- Have you ever told it to anyone before?
- If you have, where does your story begin?

- What have been the major plot complications?
- What have been the climactic moments?
- Where are you *now* in that story?
- If you have never told your spiritual story, how would you tell it?
- What would be your answers to the questions above about that journey?
- How does that story participate in the lives of your faith community?

Chapter Two: Belonging

This study of Luke begins with the question of *belonging*, especially as it applied to his Gentile readers. What kinds of listening and questions can foster a fruitful conversation with Luke's gospel about the spiritual quest for belonging? One approach might be to listen to the shape of this quest in Luke's gospel and ask, how does it challenge our understanding? What are the differences between belonging as

- option or necessity,
- right or gift,
- membership or identity?

A second approach might look at the fruitful questions that arise when we consider the vast distances between our culture and the culture to which Luke addressed his gospel. For some (not all) of us in the modern world, there is no reason to believe that individuality will not remain the center around which all of the rest of our social identities revolve. But does the familial and communal world in which Luke lived still raise important questions for us? For example:

- What are the limits of individualism?
- What does a church in relationship with Christ lose when individualism dominates?
- What aspects of our individualism might we surrender as members of the body of Christ?
- How would that surrender help us?

Finally, what it might it mean to explore our identity in the terms echoed in the words, "*Ego Christus sum* . . . I am Christ's?"

- How would it change our lives to give it the kind of weight that the young prisoner gave it?
- How would belonging of that kind order all the other kinds of belonging that shape your life?

Chapter Three: Tradition

Luke's preoccupation with his Gentile audience, along with the negative light in which he portrays the responses of Jews to the preaching of Jesus, might lead to the conclusion that Luke is either uninterested or hostile to Judaism. But nothing could be further from the truth because the theme of *tradition* is highly significant in Luke's gospel, and Jewish tradition was his tradition.

What are the questions we might want to ask about Luke's view of tradition in the sacred story? Some of the more fruitful questions might be these:
- How do I understand tradition?
- What is its character and purpose?
- How do I relate to tradition?
- Do I live in slavish dependence upon it?
- Do I live in slavish rebellion against it?
- How does slavish dependence upon or slavish rebellion against tradition make it harder to hear the voice of God?
- Where do the greatest tensions between tradition and the obligation to listen for the voice of God arise in my life?
- Can I honor tradition as God's gift and, at the same time, live with immediacy in God's presence?
- Does Luke's portrayal of Jesus' ministry help me to visualize that balance?
  Can I name a specific way in which my life might change as a result of that reflection?

Chapter Four: Authority

When the question of tradition comes to the fore, the issue of authority is never far behind. It is never just a matter of *what* we believe. It is also a matter of what we *must* believe. What parts of the tradition are required? What parts can be rejected? The following

THE GOSPEL OF LUKE

questions might arise for you as part of the conversation we have with Luke's gospel about authority:

- How do I understand authority?
- How has that understanding been shaped by experience?
- How has that understanding conditioned my response to spiritual authority?
- What is my understanding of freedom?
- How has that understanding been shaped by experience?
- How has that understanding conditioned my response to spiritual freedom?
- What are the places in the church's life and in my life that are marked by the rough water of balancing freedom and authority?

Being as specific as possible about a particular situation: can I say what a healthy balance might look like?

Chapter Five: Living at the End of Time

This chapter is about eschatology, the end of time and the coming of the kingdom of God. Living at the end of time, as Luke describes it, poses some of Scripture's most daunting spiritual questions. Concerning the time in which we live now, we might ask ourselves:

- Do I believe that my time is God's time?
- If I do, does that conviction shape my use of time?
- If I did, how would my use of time change?
- How would my attitude toward the past change?
- How would my attitude toward the future change?
- What would I do now?

Chapter Six: Living in the Here and Now

How can Christians reconcile the idea that the end is close at hand with the need to find a viable ethic for the here and now, the "in-between" time? Our own conversation with Luke about life in the here and now might fruitfully explore these questions:

- What do I think discipleship means? What does Luke tell me it means?
- Where does the word discipleship fit into my spiritual vocabulary?

- Does it find a natural place in the shape of my spiritual life?
- If not, why not? Are there rough synonyms for it that shape my thinking about the spiritual life? Or is my language for it an evasion of the responsibility that goes with belonging to the kingdom of God?
- Are there specific ways in which the character of God informs my own life?
- Are my prayers in any way devoted to prayer for the kingdom of God?

SUGGESTIONS
FOR FURTHER READING

Among the **commentaries** on the gospel of Luke written for a wider audience are: George B. Caird, *The Gospel of Luke*, Westminster Pelican Commentaries (Louisville, KY: John Knox Westminster, 1978); N. T. Wright, *Luke for Everyone* (Louisville, KY: John Knox Press, 2004); and Fred B. Craddock, *Luke*, Interpretation (Louisville, KY: John Knox Press, 1990).

The majority of treatments devoted to Luke's **Gentile context** are technical in character. One of the more accessible descriptions may be found in Luke Timothy Johnson, *The Gospel of Luke*, Sacra Pagina Series 3 (Collegeville, MN: Liturgical Press, 1991), 1–26.

For a survey of the scholarship on Luke and **Judaism**, see Joseph B. Tyson, *Luke, Judaism, and the Scholars: Critical Approaches to Luke-Acts* (Columbia, SC: University of South Carolina Press, 1999) and Bernard J. Lee, *The Galilean Jewishness of Jesus: Retrieving the Jewish Origins of Christianity*, Conversations on the Road Not Taken, vol. 1 (New York: Paulist Press, 1988).

On questions of **authority** in Luke, see Jack Dean Kingsbury, *Conflict in Luke: Jesus, Authorities, Disciples* (Minneapolis: Augsburg Fortress, 1991).

On **ethics and eschatology**, see David Tiede, *Jesus and the Future*, Understanding Jesus Today (Cambridge: Cambridge University Press, 1990).

On **discipleship** in the kingdom of God, see L. John Topel, *Children of a Compassionate God: A Theological Exegesis of Luke 6:20–49* (Collegeville, MN: Liturgical Press, 2001); Robert J. Karris, *Eating Your Way Through Luke's Gospel* (Collegeville, MN: Liturgical Press, 2006); and John Laverdiere, *Dining in the Kingdom of God: The Origins of Eucharist according to Luke* (Chicago: Liturgy Training Publications, 2007).

NOTES

1. *Prayer Book and Hymnal, Containing the Book of Common Prayer and The Hymnal 1982, According the use of The Episcopal Church* (New York: The Church Hymnal Corporation, 1986), 244–45.

Introduction to the Series

2. David F. Ford, "The Bible, the World and the Church I," in *The Official Report of the Lambeth Conference 1998*, ed. J. Mark Dyer et al. (Harrisburg. PA: Morehouse Publishing, 1999), 332.
3. For my broader understanding of authority, I am indebted to Eugene Kennedy and Sara C. Charles, *Authority: The Most Misunderstood Idea in America* (New York: Free Press, 1997).
4. William Sloane Coffin, *Credo* (Louisville, KY: Westminster John Knox Press, 2003), 156.

Autobiographical Note

5. Frithjof Schuon, *Spiritual Perspectives and Human Facts* (Bloomington, IN: World Wisdom, 2007), 144.
6. Given my own position, I find myself sympathetic to the observations of Peter M. Candler Jr. and the series to which he has recently contributed. See Peter M. Candler Jr., *Theology, Rhetoric, Manuduction, or Reading Scripture Together on the Path to God*, Radical Traditions (Grand Rapids: Wm. B. Eerdmans, 2006).

Introduction

7. Peter Berger observes, for example,

   The condition of the human organism in the world is thus characterized by a built-in instability. Man does not have a given relationship to the world. He must ongoingly establish a relationship with it. The same instability marks man's relationship to his own body.... In a curious way, man is "out of balance" with himself. He cannot rest within himself by expressing himself in activity. Human existence is an ongoing "balancing act" between man and his body, man and his world. One may put this differently by saying that man is constantly in the process of "catching up with himself." It is in this process that man produces a world. Only in such a world produced by himself can he locate himself and realize his life. But the same process that builds his world also "finishes" his own being. In other words, man not only produces a world, but he also produces himself. More precisely, he produces himself in a world.

Peter Berger, *The Sacred Canopy: Elements of a Sociological Theory of Religion* (New York: Doubleday, 1967), 5–6.

8. The fallacy—the attribution of a phenomenon with multiple causes to a single cause—is known as "reductionism."

Chapter One: Telling the Old, Old Story

9. The rendering of this story appears on a website maintained by The Monastery of Christ in the Desert in Abiquiu, New Mexico. I have been unable to identify the source, but it appears to have been adapted from an older version of the story that appears in *The Sayings of the Desert Fathers: The Alphabetical Collection,* Vol. 59, trans., Benedicta Ward (Kalamazoo, MI: Cistercian Publications, 1975): 151, para. 92.

10. Perhaps the best definition of a "God-fearer" is the one sketched by Louis Feldman, who notes that the term "refers to an 'umbrella group,' embracing many different levels of interest and commitment to Judaism, ranging from people who supported synagogues financially . . . to people who accepted the Jewish view of God in pure or modified form to people who observed certain distinctively Jewish practices, notably the Sabbath. For some this was an end in itself; for others it was a step leading ultimately to full conversion to Judaism." See Louis H. Feldman, *Jew and Gentile in the Ancient World: Attitudes and Interactions from Alexander to Justinian* (Princeton, NJ: Princeton University Press, 1993), 344.

11. For a masterful treatment of the speech and its history, see Gabor Boritt, *The Gettysburg Gospel: The Lincoln Speech That Nobody Knows* (New York: Simon & Schuster, 2006).

12. Robert Wuthnow, *After Heaven: Spirituality in America Since the 1950s* (Berkeley: University of California, 1998), 1ff.

Chapter Two: Belonging

13. See Arnaldo Momigliano and Simon Price, "Roman Religion: The Imperial Period," in *Encyclopedia of Religion*, vol. 12, ed. Lindsay Jones, 2nd ed. (Detroit: Macmillan Reference, 2005), 7911–25.

14. Ellis Rivkin, *A Hidden Revolution: The Pharisees' Search for the Kingdom Within* (Nashville, TN: Abingdon, 1978): 214–15.
15. Ibid., 72–73.
16. Interfaith conversations that focus on what we all believe also suffer another fatal flaw: they are not conversations that recognize and struggle with our differences. They sublimate or devalue the differences. Such conversations are unreal and of limited value.

Chapter Three: Tradition

17. A problem of theodicy is any situation that appears to contradict the notion that God is good, sovereign, or at work in a situation. Put another way, theodicy always asks: "If God is good, sovereign, or at work, how can this be?"
18. Blake Leyerie, *Rise of Christianity: A Sociologist Reconsiders History* (Princeton, NJ: Princeton University Press, 1996), 5.
19. Cf. the healings at Simon's house (Luke 4:38–41).
20. Some scholars characterize it as "the parable of the sowed seed." E.g., Joseph A. Fitzmyer, *The Gospel according to Luke (I–IX)*, Anchor Bible Commentary 28 (New York: Doubleday & Company, 1981), 699.
21. Fred B. Craddock, *Luke*, Interpretation (Louisville, KY: John Knox Press, 1990), 111f. Craddock observes: "Real understanding—significant learning and communication in matters of value and relationship—is antiphonal; it does not occur without response" (p. 111).
22. Cf. Amy-Jill Levine, *The Misunderstood Jew: The Church and the Scandal of the Jewish Jesus* (New York: Harper One, 2006), 87ff.
23. Abraham J. Heschel, *The Prophets* (New York: Harper & Row, 1962), 7.
24. The comment is attributed to Barbara Tober. The source is not cited.

Chapter Four: Authority

25. William J. Abraham, Jason E. Vickers, and Natalie B. Van Kirk, eds., *Canonical Theism: A Proposal for Theology and the Church* (Grand Rapids: William B. Eerdmans, 2008), passim.
26. Luke Timothy Johnson, *The Gospel of Luke*, Sacra Pagina Series 3 (Collegeville, MN: Liturgical Press, 1991), 307ff.

Chapter Five: Living at the End of Time

27. Albert Schweitzer, *The Quest of the Historical Jesus; A Critical Study Of Its Progress From Reimarus To Wrede*, (trans. William Montgomery (London: A. & C. Black, 1910, 1911; repr., Minneapolis, MN: Augsburg Fortress Publishers, 2001.

28. *Monastic Liturgy of the Hours* (Shawnee, OK: St. Gregory's Abbey, 1993), 47. The translation used is the New American Bible.

Chapter Six: Living in the Here and Now

29. See Robert J. Karris, *Eating Your Way Through Luke's Gospel* (Collegeville, MN: Liturgical Press, 2006)

30. Italics mine.

31. Johnson, The Gospel of Luke, 294.

ABOUT THE AUTHOR

Frederick W. Schmidt is an Episcopal priest and director of Spiritual Formation and Anglican Studies, as well as associate professor of Christian spirituality at Perkins School of Theology, Southern Methodist University in Dallas, Texas. He holds the Doctor of Philosophy from Oxford University, where he was also a lecturer and tutor.

Dr. Schmidt's honors include a fellowship in administrative leadership with the American Council on Education and a senior fellowship with the W. F. Albright Institute of Archaeological Research. He is also a member of the Board of Examining Chaplains of the Episcopal Church.

The series editor for the Anglican Association of Biblical Scholars Study Series, he is the author of the first book in the series, *Conversations with Scripture: Revelation*. Other books by Dr. Schmidt include *What God Wants for Your Life; A Still Small Voice: Women, Ordination, and the Church; The Changing Face of God;* and *When Suffering Persists.*

ALSO IN THE ANGLICAN ASSOCIATION OF BIBLICAL SCHOLARS STUDY SERIES

Conversations with Scripture: REVELATION

"If ever theological scholarship met the laity with grace and respect, it is here in this volume. . . . I was charmed; I was instructed; I was deeply, deeply comforted by this book. Buy it, read it, and then take it to your heart for understanding."
—Phyllis Tickle, compiler, *The Divine Hours*

"This is an important start to a most welcome series. Schmidt is a gracious and experienced teacher. He knows what false expectations his readers are likely to bring to the reading of Revelation, and offers just what we need for an encounter with the book that is honest to the text and to ourselves. . . . Schmidt's book will be widely used; and deserves to be."
—Robin Griffin-Jones, author of *The Gospel According to Paul: The Creative Genius Who Brought Jesus to the World*

Morehouse books are available from Episcopal and online booksellers, or directly from the publisher at 800-242-1918 or online at www.churchpublishing.org.

ALSO IN THE ANGLICAN ASSOCIATION OF BIBLICAL SCHOLARS STUDY SERIES

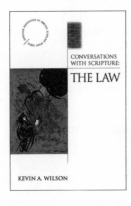

**Conversations with Scripture:
THE LAW**

"Kevin Wilson's introductory exposition of biblical Law is a must read. Unusually wide-ranging and broadly informative for a book of its size, it is jam-packed with information about the Torah's commandments, sacrifices, rituals, and theology. Wilson works hard to explain clearly how we hear God's Word today in these texts of the Law."
—Stephen L. Cook, Department of Old Testament, Virginia
   Theological Seminary

"Fresh insights into the meaning of the Law—and how Exodus and Leviticus provide guidelines for ethical behavior that helped shape a covenant community."
—*Diocesan Dialogue*, September 2006

"This addition to the series breaks new ground. This is a gem for adult education."
—*The Living Church*, November 2006

Morehouse books are available from Episcopal and online booksellers, or directly from the publisher at 800-242-1918 or online at www.churchpublishing.org.

ALSO IN THE ANGLICAN ASSOCIATION OF BIBLICAL SCHOLARS STUDY SERIES

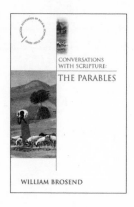

**Conversations with Scripture:
THE PARABLES**

The parables are vivid, rich, arresting stories that make us think, and teach us lessons about our relationship with God and others. From talents to mustard seeds, from shepherds to Samaritans, William Brosend shows how Jesus used common reference points to teach important truths.

 Morehouse Publishing

Morehouse books are available from Episcopal and online booksellers, or directly from the publisher at 800-242-1918 or online at www.churchpublishing.org.